Dennis Davis started canoeing on the Thames at the age of fifteen in a home-made, canvas-covered kayak. His interest in kayak design culminated in the development in the early 1960s of a round bilge kayak made from plywood without the need for moulds, jigs or building boards. This led to the development of the DK series of kayak designs which utilised this method of construction. He has since designed a small sailing dinghy for economical building by the amateur and holds the Royal Yachting Association advanced and instructor (day-boat) certificates and is a British Canoe Union senior instructor.

His publications include *The Book of Canoeing* (Arthur Barker 1969) and *The Thames Sailing Barge* (David & Charles 1970).

TEACH YOURSELF BOOKS

Canoeing

Dennis Davis

TEACH YOURSELF BOOKS
Hodder and Stoughton

First printed 1981

Published in the USA by David Mckay & Co. Inc., 750 Third Avenue,
New York, NY 10017, USA.

ISBN 0 340 24883 1

Printed and bound in Great Britain for Hodder and Stoughton paper-
backs, a division of Hodder and Stoughton Ltd, Mill Road, Dunton
Green Sevenoaks, Kent (Editorial Office; 47 Bedford Square, London,
WC1B 3DP)
by Richard Clay (The Chaucer Press) Ltd, Bungay, Suffolk

Acknowledgements

My thanks are due to all the un-named people with whom I have canoed over the years and who have given me help and advice.

For R, K and P

Contents

Introduction

Canoeing is a generic term for, as in many developing sports, various aspects of the activity known as canoeing have now evolved their own specialist techniques. As a result there are also many different canoe designs and a canoe which is competitive in one event is unlikely to be of any use for another. At the same time a marked rise in the standard of canoeing has occurred. While it is the wild water canoeing and slaloms which get television exposure it is the non-competitive canoeist paddling his own canoe quietly along a semi-disused canal or West Country estuary who forms the hidden backbone of the sport.

Throughout the following pages, therefore, the emphasis is on paddling a single seat canoe. But while learning to paddle solo with a double bladed paddle is relatively easy doing the same with a single bladed paddle is rather more difficult and instant success is less likely.

However, you can begin canoeing almost as soon as you can hold a paddle – child-sized equipment may be bought or made – and can continue long after participation in other active sports is no longer possible. The only requirement common to all canoeists is the ability to swim. This is not because the canoeist spends much time actually swimming but he does sometimes find himself tipped into cold water or even briefly inverted in his craft. It is to cope with such eventualities that swimming is so necessary. The non-swimmer is far more likely to panic, becoming a danger to himself and those trying to help, than is the swimmer who will accept an occasional ducking as an integral part of the enjoyment of canoeing rather than something to be feared and avoided at all costs.

Having written that it must be stressed that many canoeists go for years without an accidental capsize. Intentional capsize practice can be informative for the paddler as well as a good confidence builder and is discussed elsewhere in this book.

I hope you will find enough about the current canoeing world here to whet your appetite for at least one aspect of this sport – although 'sport' is perhaps a misnomer for caneoing may be undertaken as a very gentle exercise, better likened to a stroll than running – or even jogging. This merely emphasises the all-embracing nature of canoeing.

On the other hand, a glance at the contents page will show that two of the longer chapters deal with canoeing at sea, which reflects a growing arena of interest for the canoeist. This has arisen partly as a response to problems associated with access to inland waters in the UK, and particularly the white water rivers of interest to the canoeist.

Competition canoeing is given low priority here in terms of space. This is deliberate, for the aspiring competitive canoeist needs initial training appropriate to his canoeing interest if he is to develop the correct techniques and avoid the bad ones. The British Canoe Union appreciates this and has instigated a Racing Coaching Scheme with, currently, nine Regional Racing Coaches.

With this in mind, it is well worthwhile joining your local canoe club, which will usually be affiliated to the BCU. If you want to race, or join the Coaching Scheme, individual membership is necessary. The BCU controls all aspects of canoeing in this country and is affiliated to the International Canoe Federation. Regulations relating to competitive canoeing and the quoted addresses may change from time to time but the BCU will normally be able to answer any enquiry concerning canoeing. Do enclose a self-addressed and stamped envelope when writing to any of the organisations. This ensures a speedy reply and will help those who rely on membership fees for their continued existence.

Throughout this book masculine pronouns are used for convenience; the references apply equally to the feminine.

Finally, do not feel that you must start at the beginning with Chapter 1 – each chapter is intended to stand as a section in its own right and may be read as such.

1

How it all Started

Canoeing probably began when early man discovered that a floating log provided a convenient method for crossing a river. From this it was a short step to using the log for travelling *along* the river. Later man began working the log to make it more suited to his purpose as a floating load carrier. The obvious course was to shape the log by hollowing, and fashioning the ends, to give some semblance of streamlining; the end result was the crude dug-out canoe. The use of such a simple craft was limited to those areas where sufficiently large trees grew but even today dug-out canoes are in use in parts of Africa and South America.

In some coastal areas more sophisticated craft were developed with outriggers to improve stability or, sometimes, with the sides built up to give increased carrying capacity. The limitation remained the size of the available trees. Where suitable trees were not readily found different, more sophisticated, craft evolved. Of particular interest to the canoeist is the Eskimo kayak and the open canoe of the North American Indian.

At this point it would, perhaps, be sensible to define how I use the terms 'kayak' and 'canoe' in this book. In Britain we tend to refer to all craft which are pointed at both ends as 'canoes'. Then to differentiate between the open and decked varieties we call the open type 'Canadian canoes'. In this book I shall refer specifically to decked canoes *where the paddler sits with his legs outstretched* as 'kayaks', and to open types, or *where the paddler kneels in order to use a single bladed paddle*, as 'canoes'. The italic qualifications will become clear in the next chapter. Where the reference is applicable to either type, the term 'canoe' only will be used to avoid unnecessary repetition.

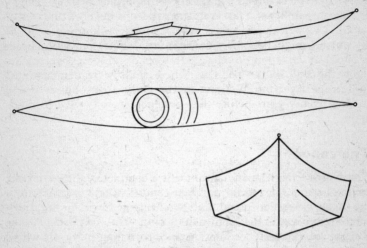

FIG. 1

Typical Eskimo kayak showing the near straight keel line; strongly curved sheer with upswept ends and the consequently long overhangs. Deck lines are indicated although the actual position of these vary according to the type of kayak and personal preferences. The end view shows the hard chine shape which is typical of the original kayaks.

The kayak

There are many different types of Eskimo kayak but all are basically similar. They are constructed of a wooden framework, covered with sealskins meticulously sewn together with stitches which do not penetrate the thickness of the skin, thus reducing to a minimum the possibility of leaks. The kayak is decked and the paddler sits in a small, rimmed cockpit into which he seals himself by fastening the lower edge of his sealskin anorak over the rim or coaming. Self-rescue is possible by rolling the kayak upright in the event of a capsize without water finding its way in.

Because the paddler sits low in the kayak, with his legs more or less flat on the bottom of the craft, he uses a double bladed paddle, paddling on alternate sides of the kayak. For this to be done efficiently the kayak has to be narrow, and consequently long, to provide sufficient buoyancy to support the weight of the paddler. This length gives directional stability – important in sea canoeing – and the possibility of a fast craft since speed is in part a function of length. A typical sea-going kayak, used for hunting seal off Greenland, might be some 5–6 metres (17–19 feet) long with a beam of about 48 cm (19 in). Such a craft depends for its sea-worthiness upon the skill of the paddler. These skills were demonstrated in Europe by Gino Watkins in the early 1930s but it was a further twenty years before they became generally used in canoe sport.

The canoe

The North American Indian canoe is a completely different craft having been developed for different conditions and uses. Whereas the kayak was designed and built as a firing platform for hunting – rather in the way of the English duck punt – the open Indian canoe is designed as a craft for long distance travelling in forests where walking can be an arduous and tedious business. The canoe is made entirely from materials available in the forest; the outer skin being of birch bark. This, after cutting to shape, was sewn to a horizontal frame consisting of wooden gunwale strips and thwarts. Into this shell thin cedar ribs were bent and jammed under the gunwale strips. The hull was then completed by forcing thin planking between the ribs and the outer skin. The seams were then sealed with natural gum.

The canoe is open, except for short strengthening decks at bow and stern. It is much beamier and deeper than the kayak to suit its role as a load carrier and it rides over waves and rapids rather than cutting through them. The original birch bark canoe varied considerably in size according to the geographical location and intended use, e.g. river canoes differ from those used on lakes. Modern versions of the canoe are typically 4.2–5.4 metres (14–18 feet) long with a beam varying between 75–105 cm (2 feet 6 in–3 feet 6 in).

The Indian uses a single bladed paddle on one side of the canoe only and, to achieve maximum efficiency, it is necessary to adopt a

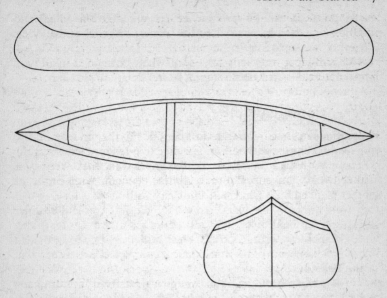

FIG. 2

Open Canadian canoe showing the beamy hull; almost straight sheer with upturned ends; short strengthening decks only, and the inward curved hull sides – tumble-home. The latter has the effect of increasing the freeboard when heeled. The end view shows the full-bodied round bilge shape.

high paddling position which enables the paddle blade to be used vertically. The Indian kneels in the canoe and this remains the most efficient way of paddling the beamy canoe.

As European settlers penetrated further into Indian country they too adopted the canoe and in time evolved new methods of building more in line with conventional European boat-building practice. Two main forms of construction came into use: the 'American', where the canoe is built with wide ribs, planked with thin boards, and covered with canvas, painted to make it waterproof; and the 'Canadian' where the canoe is all-wood, the skin being made of narrow boards carefully butted together along their length so they are watertight and further sealing unnecessary. The ribs used are narrow and closely spaced. The resulting craft is extremely attractive in its usual varnish finish. This is the type of canoe which was popular on the Thames but is less suited to the rough and tumble of rapid river work than the 'American' which, while less elegant, is easier to repair.

Both building methods are somewhat outmoded now and modern versions will be discussed later.

Recreational canoeing

Recreational canoeing began in the UK in the middle of the nineteenth century with the appearance of a form of kayak on the Thames. Although based on the Eskimo kayak, they were constructed, like conventional river skiffs, of wood with carvel or clinker planked hulls (the main similarity with the kayak being that they were decked). They differed too in being shorter and beamier than the traditional kayak, typically about 4.5 metres (15 feet) long with a beam of 75 cm (2 feet 6 in). The paddler used a double bladed paddle but the beam of the craft made its use less efficient than that of the Eskimo.

In 1866 John MacGregor, an evangelical barrister, put canoeing firmly on the map by publishing *A Thousand Miles in the Rob Roy Canoe*, an account of his travels through Europe in an all-wood decked kayak. Later he was to publish similar accounts of his canoe travels in the Baltic and in the Middle East. MacGregor subsequently founded the Canoe Club which, with the patronage of the Prince of Wales, became the Royal Canoe Club in 1873; and is still based on the Thames at Teddington. The club organised paddling races but also began to sail the kayaks. This development, however, led to their decline since the already heavy craft now became impossibly heavy with the additional weight of a centreboard case and other sailing gear. The decked paddling kayak thus became a sailing craft and evolved into the highly developed, present day International Ten Square Metre sailing canoe – one of the fastest sailing monohulls available. Although the sailing canoe is outside the scope of this book their sailing organisation remains under the aegis of the British Canoe Union (BCU).

Canoeing then declined to the status of a casual recreation using heavy wooden kayaks of the Rob Roy type and smart varnished canoes. Despite this, several more or less eccentric individuals followed the lead given by MacGregor and made canoe trips, accounts of which were sometimes published. One of the best known is that made by R. L. Stevenson in his kayak 'Cigarette' which he described in *An Inland Voyage*, published in 1890.

It was not until the beginning of the twentieth century that canoeing received its next boost when a German, Hans Klepper, began manufacturing the folding kayak. This consisted of a wooden skeleton with cross frames to determine the plan and side shape, and jointed longitudinal stringers fastening these together and forming the base for the one-piece rubberised canvas hull and canvas deck. It was an immediate success with young German enthusiasts, and by 1930 had made its appearance in the UK. By the end of the decade it was being manufactured here. In 1936 the various existing British canoe clubs amalgamated to form the British Canoe Union and in the same year a British team went to Germany for the Olympic Games, the first Games to include canoeing. Folding kayaks were used for the racing, the sport being far less specialised than it is today.

The folding kayak remained the most popular type but as it was relatively expensive the amateur enthusiast turned to the rigid, canvas-covered kayak. While these were less convenient to store and transport (except by car) they were within the capabilities of the amateur builder and large numbers were built before plywood or glass reinforced plastics construction became possible. Designs for canvas covered rigid kayaks are still available but their popularity has declined with the advent of more modern methods of construction. (A few folding kayaks remain available on the market for those requiring such a craft.)

At the outbreak of the Second World War recreational canoeing again declined. Canoes did, however, play a part in the war effort as various types were developed for clandestine operations. The most famous of these was the raid on shipping in the port of Bordeaux which is described in C. E. Lucas Phillips' *Cockelshell Heroes*. Wartime research also resulted in the development of more reliable synthetic adhesives which in turn made possible better quality waterproof plywood. A parallel development was moulded construction where thin veneers of wood are stuck together over a mould under hot or cold pressure. This gives a very light, strong craft but tends to be expensive because of the labour intensive work involved, and – in the case of hot moulding – the equipment required. Some British moulded veneer racing kayaks were made in the 1940s by the Jicwood Company and these were used for practice before the 1948 Olympic Games but were never put into large scale production. Current racing craft of similar construction are imported.

After 1945 canoeing began to grow in popularity as a competitive sport and slalom, which takes its name from the broadly similar sport in skiing, began to be taken seriously. New designs for folding and rigid kayaks, especially suited to the needs of the slalomist, appeared and some companies started marketing kits for the home

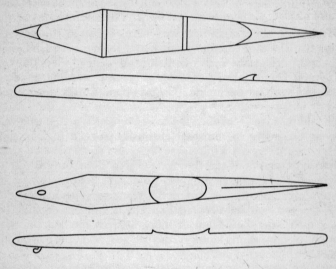

FIG. 3

TOP   *A typical C 1 sprint canoe, usually made of moulded wood veneers.*
BOTTOM   *The K 1 spring kayak which may be of GRP or veneer. The K 2 and K 4 are of similar shape.*

builder. Similarly, with the advent of the moulded veneer racing kayak, sprint racing began to take off in a way which had not been possible with the heavier, less rigid, folding kayaks previously used.

At this point the division into the specialist areas which exist today becomes apparent. The sprint kayak became longer and narrower than the folding kayaks from which it had developed; while the slalom kayak was developed to cope with the increasingly difficult courses offered by the slalom organisers; and the canoe became a strangely shaped shell for sprint racing, and grew decks for slalom. To offer the less specialised canoeist some competition, the long distance race came into being. This branch of the sport grew from the best known, and longest, British long distance race, from Devises in Wiltshire to Westminster Bridge, a distance of some 125 miles (200 km) on canal, river and tideway.

Now, even the long distance racer uses a sprint racing kayak and yet another competitive event has joined the calendar – the down river or white water race run over a relatively short course on a rapid and difficult river. In some ways it is like an extended slalom course, and requires its own specialised kayak or canoe.

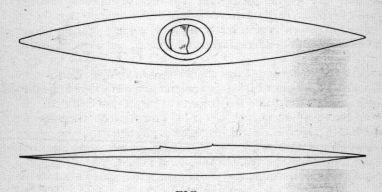

FIG. 4
A modern K 1 slalom kayak showing the hollow keel line at the ends to shorten the water line length. The coaming is recessed into the deck.

Since 1945 the growth of private car ownership has led to the decline of the folding kayak for it is just as easy to carry a couple of rigid kayaks on the roof rack as a folding kayak in the boot. Designers started experimenting with new materials and the plywood hard chine kayak was produced. These were of conventional boat construction with a light wooden frame clad with thin waterproof plywood. The British Canoe Union introduced the National Chine Kayak rules which encouraged the building of inexpensive racing kayaks. A more recent development of the hard chine kayak and canoe is the construction method where pre-cut plywood panels are 'sewn' together with copper wire and the resulting joints reinforced with glass-fibre tape and resin. Some designs have been produced using this method with more than two panels on each side. This can give an approximation to a round bilge hull shape but involves more joints and additional weight.

With the introduction of glass-fibre reinforced plastics (GRP) it became possible for the first time virtually to mass-produce craft and this method of construction is now the most common for all types of kayak and canoe. Because an expensive 'female' mould is required it is not practical for making 'one-off' craft but the amateur builder can hire a mould and make himself a GRP kayak in a long week-end if he wishes. There has been some experimenting, too, with the use of other plastics for construction but these have not proved popular, partly, I think, because of the difficulty in making a light craft which is sufficiently rigid. The same problem is encountered by the builders of larger GRP craft, such as racing sailing dinghies.

All GRP kayaks and canoes should be of round bilge design since this is perfectly practical for the construction method and gives the best strength/weight/performance ratio for the finished craft.

A similar hull shape is only possible with plywood using the DK method of construction which makes best use of the thin waterproof plywood and enables a strong, rigid monocoque round bilge hull form to be produced without the use of moulds, jigs, or building boards. In fact the hull panels have to be fastened down only while they are being scarfed together to provide the necessary length; after that the kayak may be hung from the garage roof between building sessions thus making this construction method ideal for the amateur.

Further details of the DK designs are given in Chapter 11 on construction methods.

2

Which Canoe?

Chapter 1 traced briefly the development of the modern kayak and canoe from their utilitarian forbears to the current GRP versions. How to choose from the variety of modern canoeing hardware available today is the next requirement.

Specialist canoes

An initial survey of the canoe market may surprise the newcomer as the majority of craft offered appear to be designed for the specialist, competitive canoeist. The best known manufacturers offer a variety of slalom craft, down river and wild water racing kayaks, sprint and long distance racing kayaks (usually the canoe versions of these), and often a special kayak designed for sea canoeing. Almost as an afterthought, there will be a touring kayak or canoe tucked away in the catalogue or price list. Most of these are now designed specifically for touring but only a few years ago the touring kayak was often an outdated slalom kayak. Now the more extreme design of slalom craft means they are no longer suitable for touring, and genuine touring designs are produced. Some manufacturers even tend to specialise in the supply of touring kayaks and canoes, and the choice is better today than it has been for some years past.

In spite of this you will probably find a far greater choice of competitive craft. This is not really surprising for although I suspect the majority of canoeists are non-competitive, their craft are likely to last many years – perhaps even a lifetime. In contrast, the slalom canoeist may well damage his craft beyond repair during a season, and will in any case probably require the latest 'go faster – be more manoeuvrable' boat for next year. Manufacturers obviously wish to meet this demand and tailor their production accordingly – hence the predominance of sporting craft in most maker's lists.

If you are proposing to buy a new canoe it is worthwhile visiting the annual canoe exhibition held in London at the end of Febraury. Here you will find examples of every type of kayak and canoe together with all the necessary – and some unnecessary – equipment and accessories that you require. For the canoeist this is the equivalent of the London Boat Show and represents an ideal opportunity for the newcomer to find out what canoeing is all about.

The right one for you

How, then, do you make the right choice from the multitude of craft currently available? First do you have more time available than money? If money is no problem, within reason, you will be able to buy your first craft. If you have more time than money, bear with me for a while for I shall come later to the feasibility of building your own canoe.

You will have gathered by now that your choice of craft depends very largely upon the type of canoeing you wish to take up. It is assumed at this stage that you are a first-time buyer even if you have been canoeing before.

If you are planning to enter competitive canoeing, you are well advised to visit your nearest canoe club. Talk to club members, find out what is involved and do not forget that if you are aiming for the top in this sport great dedication will be required. Your canoeing performance on the water is only the visible sign of a rigorous schedule of training. This is discussed more fully later.

However, many readers will be interested principally in buying a craft in which they can get out on the local river or canal at weekends with perhaps a longer cruise in another area during their annual holiday. This is what I call 'pottering', canoeing without any particular aim other than the entirely laudable one of being afloat in a small craft and enjoying the freedom which canoeing can give.

If this is the picture canoeing conjures up for you, do not be misled into buying a broad-beamed barge of a craft with the false idea that it will provide a safe beginning to your canoeing debut. Many people fall, all too easily, into this trap. The wide, flat bottomed kayak will, indeed, float adequately but it will be a pig to paddle and in all likelihood very heavy into the bargain.

So what should you be seeking in your first craft?

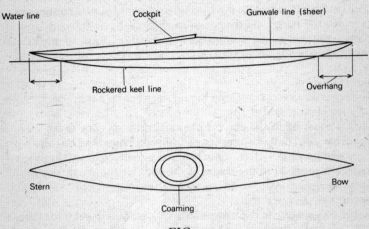

FIG. 5
A typical modern kayak labelled as the descriptions in the text.

Aspects of design

As with all things it is difficult, if not impossible, to get something for nothing, and canoeing is no exception.

Length and breadth

In general boats are faster and easier to propel if they are long and narrow – a good example is the rowing eight, which is designed and built without regard to rules other than a need to support its crew and the stress they will impose upon its structure. Exceptions are craft which are designed to plane – that is skim *over* the surface of the water when they reach a certain speed. Such designs are not generally practical for manually propelled craft such as canoes. Thus our kayak should be long and narrow if we wish to paddle it with a minimum of effort but the penalty to be paid is that such a kayak will be quite difficult to balance and, because of its long, straight keel, very difficult to turn from travelling in a straight line. It is not ideal, then, for the beginner trying to learn to canoe on a small river or narrow canal, but is excellent for the aspiring sprint racing canoeist, for once you have learned the art of handling such a thoroughbred no other type will present any problems of balance, with the possible exception of the sprint racing canoe in which the paddler kneels. The touring kayak therefore must be a compromise between the barge and the sprint racing kayak and it will be found that a suitable single seat kayak will have a length of about 4.5 metres (15 feet) and a beam of 60 cm (2 feet).

Cross-section

But specification doesn't stop here. Every boat is a thing of curves – or should be – and if the resulting craft is to be satisfactory the curves must be in the correct places. In the touring kayak we are concerned not only with ease of paddling and handling but also with the stability of our craft. This is allied closely to length and beam but even more so to the shape of the hull, or more exactly, to the cross-sectional shape, and in particular that part which will normally be under water.

If we look again at the barge-like kayak we find it is stable because it has a wide, flat bottom but it is this very characteristic which makes it hard work to paddle, and of course adds weight, which in turn adds to the effort required to move it through the water. The stability thus obtained is known as *initial stability* and is dependent upon the underwater shape being flat, or reasonably so, across the beam. If the flat section extends across a broad beam the barge-like kayak results. A flat, beamy craft may be necessary if the kayak is short simply to provide enough buoyancy to support its paddler, since a short, beamy boat will carry as much as a long, narrow one of similar underwater volume. Some initial stability is essential or the boat will not float in an upright position (a floating log is an extreme example of a vessel lacking initial stability).

A boat with a semi-circular underwater cross-section has the least amount of wetted surface and is therefore the fastest and most easily propelled shape. The problem such a shape presents is staying upright in it. To some extent this may be overcome by lowering the centre of gravity in the craft, and in the kayak this means sitting as low as possible. In a touring kayak, where space is required under the decks, this could make paddling difficult. The racing kayak, not requiring this storage space, can have a very shallow, almost round-bottomed, hull offering the maximum in speed at the expense of manoeuvrability and stability. The touring kayak must therefore compromise on hull shape too.

There are two basic designs: a flattened 'U' shaped hull cross-section which offers good initial stability and may be improved for the touring kayak by making the bottom slightly 'V' shaped. This improves the final stability and the handling characteristics in waves.

The second is one found in the DK designs which have a round bottomed 'V' shaped hull form. This has less initial stability than the 'U' shape, but enhanced stability when the hull is heeled slightly. The result is a responsive craft which handles well in most conditions.

It will now be seen that the wide, flat bottomed barge shape, which at first sight seemed very safe is not – and hard work to use as well.

Side elevation

The fourth variable is the shape, as viewed from the side. Obviously it is not possible to separate the effect of each facet of design since they interact to produce the craft the designer envisaged. We have already seen that a long craft with a straight keel line will travel easily in a straight line but will be difficult to turn, thus for manoeuvrability we shall have to shorten the kayak to reduce the waterline length. Curving the keel line along its length will also enhance manoeuvrability since it will lift the ends of the hull, thus reducing resistance to turning. This curving upward of the keel line towards the ends of the hull, called *rocker*, also enhances stability by lowering the centre of gravity.

The modern slalom kayak achieves a remarkable compromise by retaining sufficient buoyancy to cope with the weight of the paddler in rough water; enough waterline length for the paddler to be able to propel it at a reasonable speed, while being extremely manoeuvrable with a very flat hull, plenty of rocker and a low, rounded deck.

The touring kayak will require less rocker but should have some to aid turning when no rudder is fitted. Since it is waterline length which determines speed, the racing kayak has vertical ends, with no overhangs, to gain the maximum waterline length within the maximum length rule. Similarly the slalom kayak, which requires a short waterline length to aid manoeuvrability but also has a minimum length rule, has developed overhangs which are almost flat extensions of the hull and deck, the real hull shape actually starting some way in from the measured ends of the kayak. The latter is an example of the way in which competition rules may actually be contrary to the best form of craft development despite the fact that they exist ostensibly to prevent the development of impractical or unseaworthy craft.

Some normal overhang is usual on the touring kayak but should not be extreme, for the longer the overhang the more 'V' shaped the ends have to be. The alternative, spoon-shaped ends, is not ideal for speed, and while you may not be interested in speed for its own sake, a fast shape is easier to paddle. The sea-going kayak, usually based on the Eskimo kayak, often has long overhangs which are upswept to both cut through waves and to increase buoyancy in the narrow 'V' sectioned bow and stern. The upcurved ends of the sea kayak also assist in rolling the kayak after a capsize since they make it unstable in the inverted position. However, as extremes should be avoided for the normal touring kayak, the deck line should be as low as possible, commensurate with sufficient storage capacity beneath them to avoid being adversely affected by the wind.

Weight

Weight is the fifth variable to be considered and here, within reason, it is best to go for the lightest craft which suits you in every other respect. Weight depends very largely upon the method and materials of construction. Most common at present is glass reinforced plastics (GRP) which means glass fibres in the form of either random strand mat or woven cloth impregnated with polyester resin to form a laminate. While building is in progress the resin is a viscous liquid and a female mould is used. When the laminate has cured the separate parts of the craft – the hull, deck, and cockpit/seat mouldings in the case of kayaks – are trimmed and joined together with glass-fibre tape or mat and resin. The result is a strong monocoque structure with no internal framing. A GRP kayak does not need to be heavy, for an excess of resin which is what adds weight, does not add strength proportionately.

Look at the craft which interest you, and compare construction and weights. Work is currently being done on a new British

Standard for canoe construction and there is a British Canoe Manufacturers' Association to which most of the better known makers belong and which should offer some standard as to design and construction. This is not to say that a manufacturer not belonging to the Association makes poor canoes – you the buyer must make your own decision.

GRP construction

New materials are now making inroads into the established pattern of GRP construction. Polyester cloth, for example, provides a lighter, if more expensive, alternative to glass-fibre, and new resins are appearing but these are not likely to make much impression on the touring canoe for a while. Their influence is mainly in the construction of slalom and white water racing craft where high impact resistance is very desirable.

A hull which will bend when it hits a rock then return to its original shape without damage is likely to be in demand even though the penalty for this is reflected in the price which is higher than for normal GRP construction.

Local reinforcement of the GRP hull has been tried using carbon fibres. This adds greatly to the stiffness of the laminate at the possible expense of local stress points, and of course, adds to the cost. Some touring craft have spray deflectors or grooves moulded into their shape to provide stiffness (without adding weight or cost) since a 'floppy' hull sacrifices speed.

As mentioned in Chapter 1, other plastics are now used for small boat construction but so far have made little impact, largely because of the problem of obtaining sufficient stiffness at an acceptable weight. Further, capital expenditure is likely to be much higher than that required for GRP construction and, unless a very high volume of sales can be guaranteed this could prove a major drawback.

Plywood construction

The second most popular form of construction is that of plywood. Although there are several methods of making plywood kayaks only two are currently in general use and details of these are given in Chapter 14. Plywood construction offers the easiest way of building a kayak for your own use and the cost should be less than half that of a ready-made GRP kayak if you build from plans – perhaps rather more if you build from a kit. Building a GRP kayak for yourself is hardly worthwhile from the point of view of cost unless you build several craft. It is possible to hire the moulds and to buy 'kits' of glass mat, resin, etc. But to do this for one kayak is not really practical. It might be considered if several people with the same design taste club together to build themselves GRP kayaks from a hired or borrowed mould.

The canoe

The canoe offers a similar amount of choice. Although it is now becoming more popular the canoe has always lagged behind the kayak in popularity, possibly because, as a single seat craft, it is slower and more difficult to handle than the kayak single. The canoe really comes into its own as a two-person touring craft, when it is ideal. If you are prepared to master the art of single bladed paddling a solo canoe or if you have a regular paddling companion, the canoe should be considered. It is, in my opinion, a far better craft than the two-seat kayak if the paddlers have mastered the single bladed technique.

There are several GRP canoes available – one in cold moulded plywood; one kit for 'stitch and glue' plywood; and one company importing American aluminium canoes. The latter is riveted and a Canadian canoeist I know claims that they suffer from rivet corrosion. However, this problem may now have been overcome. They are, in any event, quite expensive because of import and transport costs, although they should be long-lived.

Design
Shapes vary but are, in the main, similar to the traditional North American canoe with upcurved ends and a full-bodied cross-section with a wide, flattish bottom offering plenty of initial stability and carrying capacity. You are unlikely to have much choice as to rocker, but a keel line with some rocker is better for rough water use, since it makes for good manoeuvrability. Freeboard, if not excessive, is also useful. Very high ends, however, should be avoided since these are much affected by the wind, which can render solo paddling almost impossible. In general it is probably best to go for a canoe which is not too extreme in shape. Do consider weight, too, as many GRP canoes are heavy; a fact to be considered not only when paddling but when handling ashore, too.

It is possible to have a lot of fun on the sea in an open canoe but this is not really a practical use for them except inshore in very calm weather and, since continuous calm weather cannot be guaranteed around our coasts, the serious use of the open canoe on the sea is not recommended. The addition of a full length spray deck does render them more seaworthy but this type of deck is primarily for keeping water out of the canoe when touring inland and cannot be relied on to keep the interior dry at sea.

Competitive canoes

For the sporting enthusiasts single and double slalom canoes are available in which the paddler kneels within a small cockpit, while the remainder of the canoe is decked like a kayak. The wild water or down river racing canoe is similarly decked but of a faster shape, not unlike the equivalent kayak, in fact. The sprint racing canoes are undecked shells in which the paddler kneels to paddle, and are steered largely by the paddler leaning his body. Their underwater shape is similar to that of the sprint racing kayak but, in order to conform to the rules of their class, the plan shape is of an elongated diamond with the point of maximum beam well aft to avoid interfering with the paddling action. To keep this point well above the waterline, and to avoid scooping up water, the gunwale line sweeps up to the point of maximum beam giving the craft a somewhat strange shape. This is another example of how class rules can distort the design of conforming craft. (See Fig. 3).

Your final choice then depends on your intended use. Do look at as many different types as possible, try them if you can, and discuss your requirements with other canoeists. This will probably mean joining a club – which is good idea anyway. The BCU will be able to give you details and, the address of the BCU is given in the list of addresses on p. 120.

The paddle

Whatever type of craft you choose you are going to need a paddle: for the kayak a double bladed one, and for the canoe a single bladed type. The paddle should be a personal piece of equipment, chosen to suit you and your canoe.

The double bladed kayak paddle

The double bladed kayak paddle should be of such a length that you can just tuck your fingers over the end of the upper blade when you are standing. Its length is determined both by your height and your arm length.

After length the second most important factor is weight. Remember, if you are a tourist you may be carrying the paddle at near shoulder height for several hours, quite apart from using it to propel yourself and the kayak!

Lightness, commensurate with strength, is a priority. This may be achieved in different ways and, as with canoe construction, one tends to pay for lightness when it is allied to adequate strength. The best paddles have laminated looms (shafts) and blades made from various woods. For example the loom may be made from laminations of spruce – a light straight-grained wood – and ash – a tough, springy timber. This combination is arranged to give the required weight and 'feel' to the paddle. To reduce weight further the resulting laminate may be hollow with spruce and mahogany laminated blades carefully shaped for efficiency and scarfed into the loom. There has been some scientific investigation into the most efficient shape for paddle blades and the results can now be seen in the touring paddle.

Paddles may also be fitted with shaped hand grips, or the loom shaped accordingly, to maximise paddling effort. Towards this end, too, the blades on the double ended paddle are fitted at right angles to each other. This 'feathering' reduces wind resistance of the upper blade travelling forward through the air during the paddling action, and results in a more natural and efficient paddling action.

It is important early in your paddling that you determine which way you naturally twist the loom for on this depends the way the blades face. For example, if you use your left hand to twist the loom – known as left hand 'control' – when the left blade is in position for its paddling stroke, (i.e. blade at an angle to the water and about to enter it) the right hand, or upper blade, will be facing upwards. With right hand control the upper blade will be facing downwards. You can experiment with this action by using a broom as a paddle. Obviously you should determine which 'control' suits you before buying a fixed blade paddle. It is possible to buy paddle kits which have a pair of separate blades made of plywood, or, more commonly these days, of plastics, which are then fitted into a tube of aluminium or GRP. GRP is more flexible and thus has a 'feel' more like a wooden loom. Flexibility is a matter of personal choice. Some paddlers prefer stiff paddles, others quite 'whippy' ones. If you buy a kit you can, of course, experiment with the control.

Paddles are also available in two sections with a ferrule joint in the centre. These are mainly of interest for carrying as spares when touring, especially on the sea when the loss or breakage of a paddle could literally be fatal. When the folding kayak was popular the two piece paddle was also common since its two sections were about the same length as the longest sections of the hull framework.

Blade shape

Blade shapes vary both in cross-section and in plan. The beginner will probably be well suited with a pair of flat blades of wood or plastics which can be obtained inexpensively in kit form. The flat blades avoid any problems arising from the feathering action since back and front of the blades are the same. All other blades are more or less curved along their length and may have ribs on the face or back of the blade. Racing blades may also be curved across the face, i.e. are spoon shaped.

Plan shapes vary from the almost rectangular through oval to the asymetric racing paddles designed to provide maximum effect with minimum expenditure of effort. The area of the blade relates to effort required in a similar way to the gearing on a bicycle. A blade with a large area, as used for sprint racing, is a top gear paddle which requires considerable effort if it is to be used efficiently. A smaller, narrow blade, such as that used by the Eskimo, is a low gear paddle capable of being used at a steady rate for long periods of time. Our touring blade will be a compromise – again!

The single bladed paddle

The single bladed paddle seems more simple, and in some ways this is true. The traditional method of determining the length of the single bladed paddle was to have the hand grip level with the eyes when the tip was on the ground. However this takes no account of the length of the blade, the arm length of the paddler, or the depth of the canoe, all of which should play a part in determining the effective length of the paddle.

Current thinking in America suggests that the best way of fixing the length of the paddle *loom* is to take it as the distance from the water level to your mouth when kneeling, and about 5 cm (2 in) less when sitting on a gunwale height seat. To this is added the length of the blade which should be about 60 cm (2 feet) for a general purpose paddle. The overall length of paddle achieved may be little different from that obtained by the traditional method but it does mean you obtain the correct ratio of loom to blade length for you and your canoe.

American research on the single blade has produced the bent paddle loom. The loom is laminated and bends backwards at about 15 – 18° from a point about 5 cm (2 in) above the blade. This provides a more efficient paddling action, but it does make some of the traditional single blade strokes difficult, if not impossible. If you fancy trying the bent loom paddle you will have to make your own since they are not as yet available in Britain.

Apart from racing paddles, which have curved blades similar to those used for kayak racing, the blades of most single bladed paddles are flat. Variations occur in the size and shape of the blades, the shape of the grip at the top of the loom, and the materials from which they are made.

Generally the materials used are the same as for kayak paddles. The all-wood paddle is more responsive but also more expensive than the composite wood or plastics blade with an aluminium or GRP loom. The plastics and aluminium single bladed paddle seems somehow less pleasant than its double bladed counterpart but this is a purely personal feeling and they are certainly less expensive.

You can make simple versions of either type of paddle and further details on this are given in Chapter 14.

The baths kayak

There is one type of kayak which I have so far omitted – the baths kayak. This was a deliberate omission because I am not convinced that canoeing is, or should be, an indoor sport. However, to complete the picture: the baths kayak is short – usually about 2.4 metres (8 feet) with a cross-sectional shape similar to that of a slalom kayak, but with a more rectangular plan shape, this being necessary to provide sufficient carrying capacity and longitudinal stability. The main use, as the name suggests, is for canoe practice in swimming baths and for canoe polo. There is no doubt that a lot of fun can be had in a baths kayak – the experienced can loop them and even dive-bomb from the diving boards. But, this said, I still feel that canoeing should be an opportunity to get to grips with nature in a purely personal way which suits you. If you want to paddle a baths boat in a swimming bath a couple of nights a week, why not?

The knowledgeable will be thinking that the surf shoe has not been mentioned; it will be.

3

Safety Aspects

The best safety measure the canoeist can adopt is proficiency. As we shall see later, there are a number of different paddle strokes the canoeist uses and it is the way in which he combines these to suit the prevailing situation which marks the degree of proficiency attained.

Watch a top slalom paddler and you will understand this, but you will have to watch carefully for his different paddling movements will tend to merge into each other so that the individual strokes are almost indistinguishable.

But notice too that he will be wearing a bouyancy aid, probably a protective jacket or anorak (perhaps over a wet suit) and a protective helmet. Since the kayak or canoe will be under water almost as much as on it the cockpit will be covered by a spray cover which fits tightly around the canoeist and around the rim of the cockpit. This effectively seals the interior and lets the canoeist roll his craft upright again in the event of a capsize.

You may be wondering what this has to do with paddling on the local canal in a touring single, with never a thought of wild water. Plenty! for in canoeing, as in every activity, it always pays to be prepared for all eventualities. It's a form of insurance if you like, and inexpensive for the value obtained.

The buoyancy aid

The slalomist usually wears a *buoyancy aid* in the form of a vest with closed cell foam or air-filled sacs sewn into tubes of nylon or similar material. As this is relatively slim it does not hinder the paddling action while at the same time it provides both protection for the body and some insulation against cold although the latter may be a disadvantage in some situations. The buoyancy aid, as its name suggests, is an aid only in the event of the canoeist having to abandon his canoe. It will not save an unconscious paddler.

The life-jacket

The *life-jacket*, when properly used, will keep an unconscious person is such a position that he can breathe. The type commonly used by canoeists, and approved by the BCU, is the two stage type, which has inherent buoyancy of at least 6 kg ($13\frac{1}{2}$ lb), and with provision for oral inflation to increase the buoyancy to a maximum of about 18 kg (40 lb). The inherent buoyancy is such that it 'shall support the trunk of the wearer at an angle inclined backwards from the vertical' (BS 3595). When fully inflated it '. . . shall automatically turn an exhausted or unconscious person . . . so that the mouth of the . . . person is held well clear of the water with the trunk of the body inclined backwards . . . .' It must do this within five seconds and must not allow the wearer to remain face downward. In addition, the jacket must be fitted with a rot-resistant harness, a lifting becket clearly positioned at the front, and have a non-metallic whistle secured to it. Its materials and construction are subject to a number of tests before it can receive the British Standard Kite mark, so if you buy such a jacket you are reasonably assured of its quality. Because the British Standard applies to a number of different types of life-jacket do make sure that the one you buy is suitable for canoeing. A recognised canoe stockist will help you. Or the BCU will supply details of 'approved' styles on request.

Children should *always* wear a life-jacket of approved British Standard type (BS 3595). Explain its correct use to them so they know how the inflation system works. They must be actively discouraged from chewing the end of the inflation tube or its cap which is necessary for deflating the inflatable section! The gas inflated type is not recommended for canoeing and the automatically inflating type has no place in a canoe since it could inflate at just the wrong moment! The orally inflated two-stage life-jacket really is the best choice.

Occasions when wearing a life-jacket are a disadvantage are rare. The most commonly quoted is the after effects of a capsize immediately below a weir. This is dealt with on p. 60.

The protective helmet

As the term 'canoeing' includes a number of very different activities only having in common the fact that they are performed in a small boat which is pointed at both ends, it is inevitable that some equipment is more appropriate to one aspect of the sport than to others. The *protective helmet* is one such item. In design it is a light shell with holes to allow water to escape easily. The interior harness and fastenings are made of webbing, which will not hold water and dries quickly. The metal fittings should be non-ferrous and, prefarably, not of aluminium since this corrodes quickly in salt water. A helmet is essential for the slalomist and white water canoeist and may well be sensible for use on the sea especially when the launch or landing is through surf. However, it is unnecessary and inappropriate on a canal or flat water river. In other words, if you capsize in water where there are rocks or a beach on which you could hit your head then wear a helmet. If you take part in white water competition you will have to wear one; at other times, use your common sense.

The spray cover

The *spray cover* is also essential for white water and sea use, for without it your canoe will rapidly become swamped. When you buy your kayak get the spray cover at the same time. If you are building a kayak either make, or have made to measure, a spray cover which will help keep you warm and dry below the waist, even on a canal. Designs and materials vary but they all do the same job although comfort and efficiency may vary.

You must be able to remove the cover from the cockpit coaming quickly and easily if you capsize and need to leave the cockpit, i.e. if you are unable, or do not intend, to roll upright. This may take the form of a strap across the front of the cover which can be grasped to pull the cover from the coaming. In the event of your 'abandoning ship' stay with the boat unless-it is heading into danger, e.g. towards a weir. Assuming it has buoyancy at each end, it will float and, especially at sea is more easily seen than you alone – but not much more so avoid this situation!

The buoyancy

The *buoyancy* in the canoe should be *fixed* at each end so it cannot become loose and tangle with your legs. In most canoes solid, expanded-polystyrene buoyancy blocks are the best choice if they can be kept firmly in place. A good alternative, and one which I favour, is the inflatable buoyancy bag. This, ideally, is shaped to fit into the ends of the canoe and is fitted with long inflation tubes so that they can inflated on the spot, if necessary. They may be entirely air filled or like the life-jacket a combination of air and closed cell foam plastics. This type is safer since you remain protected to some extent if the bag develops an air leak. If bags are used they must be securely fastened in place.

There should be a minimum of $13\frac{1}{2}$ kg (30 lb) buoyancy at each end so the canoe will float on an even keel even when swamped. Foamed *in situ* polyurethane foam cannot be recommended since it may absorb water during use, and has been known to work free at inconvenient times. It also gives off noxious fumes while foaming.

The footrest

Also fastened firmly in place must be the *footrest*. This is an essential piece of equipment for efficient paddling in most kayaks. There are exceptions where the shape of the deck may make it more comfortable to press the feet on the floor of the hull. However, the footrest is also an item which may be considered as safety equipment because, in certain circumstances, it could save your life.

I know of two canoeing fatalities where the paddler has become jammed in the kayak feet first, unable to extricate himself or be saved by rescuers, and has drowned. This type of accident is preventable if the footrest is strong enough to support the weight of the paddler being propelled forwards when the kayak hits an obstruction in a rapid river, or the beach in surf conditions; and large enough to prevent the feet being forced alongside the footrest where they can jam. The safety footrest must therefore be both strong – and adjustable if more than one person is to use the kayak – and must fit closely into the hull.

An alternative to this platform type is a footrest of the horizontal bar type which cannot move forwards but will release when pulled backwards. This is less satisfactory for it is still possible for the body to slip forwards and jam into the bow section of the kayak, but it does facilitate external rescue if this happens.

Painters and deck lines

Externally your canoe should have *painters, deck lines* or *short lengths of rope with toggles* attached, fastened to each end. Which of these you have depends to some extent upon the type of craft – slalom types usually have toggles because the GRP canoe is a slippery thing to hold, especially when it is wet. Rope and toggles give the paddler something to hang on to when he is in the water alongside his craft. Rope loops can also be used but are not recommended as they can trap the fingers if the canoe is turned over and over in surf or rapids. Toggles are safer.

Deck lines serve the same purpose and are simply painters which are led over the decks – tightly, and clear of the cockpit – so you have something to hold in the event of a capsize. They can be arranged with loops and toggles so that they double as painters, but this may not be entirely satisfactory since they are likely to become too loose to serve as deck lines.

The traditional painter should be at least the length of the canoe and fixed one at each end. If they are not arranged as deck lines they should be tucked away where they cannot become entangled with your feet and legs if you capsize. For the tourist painters are essential.

Capsize practice

Do not be put off by all this writing of capsizes, it is possible to canoe for years without ever leaving your craft involuntarily. However, as part of the 'be prepared' philosophy it is well worthwhile finding out just how your canoe behaves when it is pushed to the limit of its stability. Pick a warm day and a safe place on a quiet river or lake for some practice capsizes. If you take a beginners' course at a club or training organisation one of the first practical exercises will usually involve a capsize. This is a great

confidence builder as it proves that it is pretty well impossible to become stuck in the cockpit of an inverted kayak. Getting 'stuck' sometimes concerns beginners and is a quite unnecessary fear. Do, of course, have help near by if you are practising informally; a companion in a wet suit standing alongside is ideal.
Try this:

1 Check that you have enough water so your head is not going to hit the bottom – or any other obstruction.
2 Place your paddle in the water on one side and capsize the other way.
3 Remain in the cockpit and reach around the hull with both arms so you can bang on the bottom of the canoe with your hands. This is a recognised 'help' signal.
4 Release your spray cover and do a forward roll out of the cockpit, coming up alongside your canoe.
5 Retrieve your paddle and swim with both to the nearest bank. Hold the canoe by the toggle or rope at the end and *do not* try to turn it upright as it will fill with water and be very difficult to handle. (While inverted the air trapped inside will keep it floating high in the water and prevent it filling so long as the cockpit coaming remains below water level.)
6 With your companion at one end of the kayak, and you at the other, gently lift the kayak to break the air lock in the cockpit. Water will run out and you should tilt it from end to end in turns until all the water has escaped.
7 Turn the canoe upright and put it back on the water.

If you are practising alone you can use the bank as a substitute for a companion, but choose a low bank or you will allow too much water to get in.

Far more care is necessary if the kayak has filled with water (it should still remain afloat because it has built-in buoyancy). Invert it in the water if it has turned upright and, again with a companion, lift from the ends but at the same time twist slightly so the water can run out without creating an airlock. Do not try to lift straight upwards or you risk breaking the back of the kayak.

Again you can do this by yourself. With the kayak inverted, stand by the cockpit and lift so that the water can run out, when most is out turn the kayak upright, go to one end and push down so the water remaining inside runs to your end, now lift and invert the kayak so the water runs from the cockpit. This has to be done in one smooth, quick movement if the water is not to run alongside the cockpit to the other end. Repeat until the kayak is emptied.

Swimming with the canoe is usually easiest if you take the upstream end (assuming you are on a river) and use a backstroke to get to the bank. In rocky conditions, where it may be impossible to go directly to a bank, allow the canoe to float in front of you and go feet first to protect your head from rocks. It is in these conditions that you will be pleased to be wearing a protective helmet.

Be comfortable

Another important factor in considering safety aspects is the matter of comfort. Basically you will be a better canoeist if you are comfortable in your seat with the footrest correctly set for you and no parts of the canoe or equipment in a position where they can chafe or cause other irritation.

The seat

Generally, kayaks are fitted with moulded GRP seats which are fixed both in position and shape so there is little to be done other than making sure before you buy that the seating arrangements suit you. If you are making your own craft it is possible to buy ready-made GRP seats or you can make a simple plywood one. With either, it is better to have a hard, shaped seat rather than a soft one, such as a cushion. This is less firm and, at the end of a few hours' paddling, will seem harder and more uncomfortable than a moulded GRP type. Seats can be made to measure by sitting in a bowl filled with damp sand. Place a sheet of Perspex, softened in hot water, over the resulting personal shape and sit on it! The Perspex shape can be fixed to a suitable wooden frame to suit the kayak concerned.

In canoes there may be seats set high near the gunwales or there may only be thwarts to lean on while kneeling on the floor of the canoe. Kneeling is the most efficient position for paddling with the single bladed paddle but the beginner may find it very uncomfortable at first. This can partly be overcome with knee pads. Since there is more scope for changing position in the canoe it is probably rather easier to remain comfortable for long periods of paddling.

Clothing

The next consideration is keeping warm and dry – the latter sometimes more difficult to achieve than the former. If you are strictly a smooth water, summer canoeist there are few problems for a waterproof anorak worn over your spray cover will protect you during summer rain. Exercising in waterproof clothing causes perspiration inside the impervious skin of the anorak which wets clothing worn underneath. However, this wetness will be warm and is better than becoming wet and cold from exposure to rain and wind. Materials are now coming on to the market which overcome this problem to some extent but they cost a lot more than the common proofed nylon or cotton anoraks.

Hypothermia

If you choose to do your canoeing in rough water, at sea, or in the winter then you must take greater care for the human body is very susceptible to cold and hypothermia can set in very quickly. In 10 – 15° C (50 – 60° F) a person dressed in light clothing (as for normal canoeing) can expect to become exhausted or unconscious within two hours and have a survival time of about six hours. At lower temperatures the survival time falls dramatically and it is worth remembering that the sea temperature around the British coasts is rarely higher than 15° C (60° F) even in the summer.

Should it be impossible to get out of the water survival time is increased if the victim remains immobile in his life-jacket since movement accelerates heat loss into the surrounding water. The effect of wind and temperature combined gives a chill factor such that even when the person is removed from the water body heat loss will continue, particularly in windy conditions, unless preventive action is taken. A large, plastic 'survival bag' should always be carried. The victim should be placed in this *in his wet clothes* if no change of clothing is available and further help sought immediately.

The wet suit

Currently the easiest way of keeping warm when canoeing in potentially hazardous conditions – and these would include any form of canoeing undertaken during the winter months in Britain –

is to wear a *wet suit*. This is now a fairly common garment used in several water sports and by those whose work takes them into cold water. There are a large number of different styles but they all insulate by fitting tightly. Any water which finds its way inside is rapidly warmed by the body. The basic material from which the suit is made is neoprene in thicknesses from 3 – 6 mm; and is usually lined with nylon in either smooth or towelling finish to aid getting the suit on and off. Some also have a nylon skin on the outside but this is a matter of fashion rather than added efficiency. The type you choose for canoeing is a matter of personal choice, but do consider the physical movement involved in canoeing and get a suit which does not chafe the arms or shoulders when paddling. I recommend the 'long john' type which is a one piece suit with long legs but no arms. They are available with a zip front or a shoulder fastening and for the canoeist, the zip front is probably the more convenient. Should you wish to canoe in extreme conditions you can then wear a jacket over the long john. You can make a wet suit, either from scratch or from a kit, but I suspect that the life of such a suit is likely to be much less than a shop bought one.

For those who cannot get used to the wet suit it may be worth investigating the effectiveness of the nylon and acrylic pile clothing which is becoming popular for sailing and other outdoor activities.

Safety in canoeing, as in many activities, is largely a matter of being prepared for the worst in order to gain the fullest enjoyment. Become proficient and you will enjoy your canoeing more and be safer. Be comfortable and this will help you stay proficient and be safer. Make sure that you and your canoe are properly equipped for what you are about to undertake and you should never end up as a coroner's statistic.

4

Where to Canoe

One of the problems facing the canoeist is where he can actually go canoeing in Britain. This arises because most stretches of suitable water in Britain are privately owned and the canoeist does not have any right to go on it. There are exceptions where there is a statutory or longstanding right of navigation; these include the Thames, Trent, Severn, Stratford Avon, Suffolk Stour, Great Ouse, Wye, and Medway – but not necessarily the whole length of the river in each case. It may also be necessary to purchase a licence, for example, on the Thames, Stratford Avon and Wye.

Rivers

Most other non-tidal rivers belong to the riparian owners (i.e. the owners of the land through which the river flows). If an owner owns only one bank of the river he has riparian ownership over the half of the river nearest his land. Many landowners dispose of the fishing rights on their section of river to angling clubs or groups, and anglers, in general, object strongly to canoeists passing along the private water they have rented or bought. This is particularly so in game fishing rivers which also tend to be the rivers of most interest to the sporting canoeist.

It is here that some difference in need is found between the competitive and touring canoeist. The organisers of slaloms and white water races are reasonably content to obtain access to suitable water on relatively few occasions during the year, which may be outside the fishing season (i.e. in winter). The tourist, by contrast, requires access to water for longer periods and when the weather is more conducive to canoe touring. This generally coincides with the fishing season. Thus the tourist is limited for the most part, if he wishes to canoe legally, to those parts of rivers where there is a statutory right to navigate, the tidal stretches of rivers, or those rivers where he can obtain special permission to canoe either personally or via the BCU.

However, this is not the whole story for even where there is a legal right to navigate there is not necessarily a legal right of access *to* the river. In other words, you have to launch your canoe only at points of public access to the river, such as a public landing stage or a ford, or by making a private arrangement with the riparian owner. The same limitation applies to camping on the bank. You must obtain permission from the landowner first! While canoeing is legal on the tidal sections of most rivers, the limitation on access to the river is still applicable. The same situation applies to lakes. Some, such as Windermere, are usable as of right but most are privately owned and permission must be sought for access to them. A disputed case taken to the House of Lords confirmed a right to canoe on the Spey (a salmon river) in Scotland.

This case has let canoeists show that they can use a salmon river without spoiling the fishing. It can only be hoped that other rivers will now be opened to our use without detriment to other users. It must surely be only a matter of time before we come into line with our European neighbours where most rivers are legally available for canoeing as they are too, for the most part, in the USA and Canada.

The BCU has been fighting the access battle for a number of years. The problem is that in most instances they are fighting against existing law which is firmly on the side of the riparian owner. In the long term only a change in the law can resolve the problem for the canoeist, who is the least polluting of all recreational water users.

The BCU has an Access Committee which is concerned with the overall organisation of this aspect of canoeing within the legal limitations currently imposed. Limited success has been achieved in making agreements with riparian owners and fishing interests on various rivers. It may be expected that such arrangements, usually offered to BCU members only, will be extended in the future until a change in the law comes into being. Details of such river agreements are available to individual members and affiliated clubs.

The BCU also has a number of River Advisors who have current information on access to the Rivers in their areas. For example, if you wish to canoe down a particular river and want to start in the upper reaches the local River Advisor will be able to tell you whether this is legally possible and when. If permission is required he will be able to tell you whom to contact. He will also be able to advise on the best place to begin with regard to the amount of water in the river, and where public access is possible.

I have deliberately painted a somewhat black picture since this problem is not going to disappear overnight unless there is a change in the law. But canoeists do still manage to find suitable water. However do remember the problems and treat all other water users – especially anglers – with courtesy. It would be a great asset if they were on our side!

Canals

You generally require a licence to canoe on a canal and the BCU has made special arrangements for its members wishing to buy a British Waterways Board licence. This covers most of the canals in Britain and includes the canalised sections of the rivers Severn, Trent, Lea and Soar.

Since they have no current other than that induced by the locks canals are not always desirable for the canoeist. Many, however, cross remote and beautiful parts of the country, which may be inaccessible to other forms of transport, and as such are very worthy of consideration by the canoe tourist.

Sea and tidal estuaries

Finally, we come to those most accessible waters in Britain, the sea and tidal estuaries. Access to tidal rivers and estuaries may present problems but, for the most part, there are points of public access where launching is possible so this is less of a problem than that presented by non-tidal rivers.

On tidal waters, and the sea itself, you are free to canoe where you like unless subject to Ministry of Defence restrictions, for example when firing ranges are in use. Landing is permissible anywhere below high water level. Above this may be private property but in general exception is not taken to canoeists landing or launching if the usual countryside courtesies are observed. You may be asked to pay for the privilege of launching, canoeing or landing within the confines of the harbour.

Other waters

In Ireland, which provides some excellent canoe touring, access to suitable canoeing water is less of a problem.

Access to water for canoeing practice is likely to be easier than has been suggested so far, for all that is required is a stretch of water which is of sufficient area to permit the canoe to be paddled forwards and backwards, and deep enough for the paddler to capsize without hitting his head on the bottom – less than one metre will be sufficient.

Your local canoe club probably has access to a suitable stretch of water or may even run beginners' lessons at the local swimming pool. This may not be a bad place to learn, especially if you are starting in the winter! Usually the Pool Superintendent will insist on special canoes being used to avoid river debris being brought into the pool. He may even be able to offer storage facilities for the canoe between sessions – this has been done in my local swimming pool. The pool is hired for an hour or so after the end of the normal public swimming session and may be shared with another compatible group, such as scuba divers, to reduce the cost.

It may also be possible to obtain permission to use a gravel pit at week-ends when it is not being worked. Do explore it thoroughly first, though, for the detritus of gravel working, e.g. discarded equipment.

5

On the Water

Canoeing, like every other sport, is best learnt by practising under the eye of an experienced tutor. In this way you will quickly learn the basics of handling a kayak or canoe. Perhaps the most satisfactory way of learning is by taking one of the short courses arranged by outdoor centres such as Plas y Brenin. Additional reading about the handling of a canoe will be of considerable help though. In this chapter we shall look at the basic handling techniques, assuming that the paddler is solo.

Launching

It is best to begin on a quietly flowing river, or a lake with a landing stage or bank about level with the coaming of the kayak or gunwale of the canoe.

The kayak

The handling of the kayak will be discussed first.

When you are ready to launch, check the buoyancy at both ends and that the toggles or deck lines are correctly fitted. Pick up your kayak by the cockpit coaming and place it in the water with the bow facing upstream in a river, and ensure that your paddle is near at hand. Let us assume that the starboard (right) side of the kayak is next to the bank. To get into the kayak, hold the front of the coaming with the left hand (the right hand remains firmly on the

bank) and put the left foot on to the centre of the floor, near the front
of the cockpit, keeping your weight on the right foot and hand on
the bank. Transfer the right foot to the cockpit, behind the left foot,
and slide your bottom on to the seat (the right hand retains contact
with the bank).

Now make yourself comfortable. Adjust the footrest if necessary.
(If this is not possible afloat get out by reversing the embarking
procedure, adjust the footrest, and start again.) Assuming all is well
fasten your spray cover, if one is worn, and you are ready to paddle
away.

In some kayaks with short cockpits it will be necessary to
straighten your legs to enter the cockpit. In this case first lower your
bottom on to the back of the coaming and slide forwards into the
cockpit. If both you and the kayak are in shallow water – i.e. up to
about knee level – place the paddle across the rear deck just behind
the cockpit, hold it in place with both hands, one each side of the
cockpit. Place the nearest foot in the centre of the cockpit, as far
forwards as possible. It is now necessary to balance the kayak while
bringing in the second foot and sliding on to the seat. If the paddle
blade on the side from which you are embarking is kept horizontal
to the water it will provide a little 'lift' if the kayak tips that way.
Success – as opposed to a capsize – is ensured by making the entry
swift and smooth.

These are suggestions only. You may see other methods which
seem preferable to you, so do try them and use the one which you
find easiest and most successful.

You are now safely embarked. Your spray cover is correctly fitted
with the release strap arranged at the front where you can get at it if
need be. The footrest is comfortable, enabling you to press your
knees against the underside of the deck to give you a firm, three
point 'fixing' in the kayak – bottom on the seat, feet on the footrest,
and knees under the deck, you and the kayak are as one and can work
together. Good paddling technique depends upon your being
positioned like this and not wobbling about.

Paddling forwards

To propel a boat forwards the ideal is for the propulsion unit to be
on the centre-line to ensure that no turning movement is introduced. In a canoe this is not possible so the canoeist has to achieve
as near the ideal as he can by keeping the paddle blade as near

the centre line as the shape and size of his craft allows. Each time the paddle blade is placed in the water and pressure exerted upon it the craft will move in the opposite direction; thus if the paddler *pulls* on the paddle the kayak will move forwards. Ideally, the paddle blade will remain static in the water and all the energy will go to moving the kayak forwards. In practice, of course, the blade will be moved through the water too. In general it will be seen that the more vertical the paddle blade, the more efficient the paddling stroke.

To find the correct position for the hands on the paddle shaft or loom hold the paddle horizontal above your head with your hands positioned so that your elbows make an approximate right angle. This is the correct position for your hands – but may be modified slightly for comfort – for all the paddle strokes described in this chapter. The paddle should be held in front of the body at about chest height so that the arms are almost horizontal from the shoulder during the paddling action. Begin the action by leaning forward slightly, and placing the left blade in the water near the side of the kayak with the left arm straight out from the shoulder (The left hand will be lower than the shoulder to allow the blade to enter the water.) Push forward with the right arm, fingers loose on the loom, and pull back with left arm. When the left blade reaches a point in the water about level with your body flick it from the water and repeat the stroke on the right. In flicking the left blade from the water you will have twisted the paddle to bring the right blade into the correct position for its stroke. This action may be practised 'dry', sitting on a stool. Keep a relaxed grip on the loom and do not allow the body to move backwards and forwards with the paddling movements as this alters the trim of the kayak and wastes energy. Avoid rocking the kayak from side to side for the same reason. Practise forward paddling like this until the correct action is automatic.

Stopping

Once you are able to paddle forwards with some degree of confidence you will need to know how to stop, how to turn, and how to bring yourself alongside a bank or another craft. Essentially stopping the kayak is achieved by paddling backwards although from slow speeds it may only be necessary to place the blades in the water at the correct angle for them to act as brakes. With the kayak moving forwards at a reasonable speed, place one blade in the water next to the cockpit, *with the blade the same way round as for forward paddling*, push the blade forward, and before the kayak has a chance to turn repeat the stroke on the other side. Ensure that the blades are at right angles to the water flow. If the lower edge is allowed forward the blade will try to dive and could capsize you. When this stopping movement has been mastered, and you are able to bring your kayak to a stop in a straight line, increase the power by putting the blades in the water *behind* the cockpit. As confidence increases you will be able to stop in a very short distance.

Paddling backwards

Paddling backwards is achieved by virtually the same stroke but can be made more effective by leaning backward and twisting the body to enable the blades to enter the water nearer the stern. *Do not* turn the blades from the normal paddling position, i.e. use the *back* of the blades for stopping and backward paddling.

Turning

Simple turns can be made by placing the blade in the water next to the cockpit as for stopping, and holding it there. The kayak will tend to turn around the blade, i.e. if the left blade is used the kayak will turn to the left. If the kayak tends to turn during normal paddling this can be corrected by paddling a little harder on the opposite side. If the paddle is constantly used as a rudder to correct minor deviations progress forwards will be very slow.

You should now be able to come alongside a bank or another craft in a perfectly satisfactory manner using your forwards and backwards paddling skills. It should never be necessary to fend off with a paddle or otherwise allow the paddle to come into contact with the bank. On a river turn to face upstream and paddle towards the bank at a slight angle. At the point where you wish to land and before the bow actually hits the bank a back paddling action on the river side will swing the bow away from the bank and, if you have judged correctly, you will be within reach of the bank and will have stopped. It is better to approach upstream as it will then be the bow which the flow of water will tend to deflect and as this is more readily seen it can easily be corrected. For the same reason it is advisable to leave with the bow facing upstream. If there is much current it is possible to move the kayak into the stream by simply placing the paddle blade in the water, on the river side of the kayak, at a slight angle to the hull. The pressure of the water flowing past the blade will force the kayak out from the bank. This should be used with discretion though for in fast flowing water the wrong blade angle could result in a capsize.

You will have already discovered that turning is easy. In fact, if you are learning in a slalom type kayak you will have found paddling in a straight line is more difficult! The most efficient way of making a simple turn is by using a *sweep stroke* on the opposite side in the course of normal paddling. Instead of bringing the blade straight back, sweep it away from the hull at the beginning of the stroke, curving in towards the hull as it is withdrawn from the water. The turn will be tighter if the normal stroke on the other side is simultaneously made less efficient by not immersing the blade fully in the water. If a tight turn is required, within the width of a river for example, a more forceful sweep stroke may be used where the paddle loom is kept low near the deck of the kayak and the blade swept well out in an arc away from the hull and withdrawn near the stern. This *bow sweep stroke* can be combined with a *stern sweep stroke* on the other side. Place the blade in the water near the stern and sweep forwards in an arc away from the hull again but this time to withdraw near the bow. The two strokes combined will turn the kayak within its own length.

It is worth experimenting with your own kayak to find which way it turns when it is leaned while moving in a straight line. Some turn away from the lean, others towards it; it depends on their under-water shape.

Avoiding a capsize

There are two strokes with which to combat the unintentional capsize. The first is known as the *slap support* although this is not a true descriptive name as the stroke is more in the nature of a 'pull-up' than a slap. To practise, lean the kayak to one side with the paddle held in the normal position with the blade on the side of the lean, face downwards. Slap the blade down on the water to regain balance. The slap should be made with the wrist dropped, so that, as the lean is advanced further, the paddler is effectively pulling up on the paddle rather than merely slapping down on the water. Practise on both sides and, as confidence increases you will be able to pull up from having your shoulder in the water. Recover by flicking the blade through ninety degrees to remove it from the water. Recovery from extremes of lean – e.g. with the head in the water – is made easier if you flick upwards with your hip at the same time as pulling up against the resistance of the paddle blade.

Similar to the slap support is the *draw stroke* which has the effect of moving the kayak sideways. Put the blade in the water as near vertical as you can with the face of the blade towards the kayak and about 30 cm (12 in) away from the hull; the upper arm should be extended almost horizontally. Push with the upper arm and pull with the lower and the kayak will move towards the blade. Just before the blade reaches the hull, twist it through ninety degrees and slice the feathered blade back to the starting position and repeat until you have the kayak where you want it. It is also possible to angle the blade during the draw stroke to pull either the bow or stern sideways to a greater or lesser extent. In practice it is common in rough water to use a form of this stroke as a support, but it must be emphasised that both the slap and draw are essentially dynamic strokes which must be carried through wholeheartedly if they are to be successful.

The second support stroke is the *sculling support*. All sculling strokes use a continuous movement of the paddle blade rather than a single dynamic action as in the slap and draw strokes. In sculling for support the paddle is held in the normal way and the blade to be used is placed face down on the surface of the water, then tilted slightly so that the edge of the blade nearest the stern is lifted. Pull the blade across the surface towards the stern and, at the same time, press down on it. At the end of the stroke tilt the blade in the opposite direction, i.e. lift the edge nearest the bow, and push it forwards over the surface. The arc travelled by the blade is quite short and the action, once learned, should be quite rapid. Having mastered the action you can lean on to the blade and you will find you can support yourself shoulder under – and further – if you combine recovery with a hip flick. With some curved or spoon-shaped blades it may be found easier to practise this stroke with the back of the blade facing downwards.

The same action provides the *sculling draw* stroke. Instead of having the blade horizontal, acting on the surface of the water, place it in the water vertically as for the draw, but rather nearer the hull. Angle the blade so that the edge nearer the stern is turned a little away from the hull and move the blade through the water towards the stern. Twist to bring the edge nearer the bow away from the hull and move it towards the bow. As this is repeated, the kayak will move towards the paddle blade. It is important to retain the normal grip on the paddle and to ensure that the face of the blade is always towards the hull. Practise all strokes on both sides of the kayak until they come spontaneously.

Canoe strokes

Canoe strokes are similar in many instances to those used by the kayak paddler who has adapted traditional canoe strokes to suit his double bladed paddle. Using the single bladed paddle has always been rather more sophisticated than double bladed paddling if only because keeping control is more difficult. The basic stroke with the single blade is designed to both propel the canoe forwards and keep it on a straight course without constantly changing sides every few strokes.

Launching
Embarking in the canoe is less of a problem than with the kayak for, with its extra beam and generally flatter hull, it is more stable. The solo paddler will be kneeling in the canoe with his bottom resting against the 'centre' thwart, which should be positioned nearer the stern than the centre. Using the sculling draw described above move the canoe away from the bank.

Paddling forwards
Once clear, place your blade in the water forward of where you are kneeling and a little away from the hull. Have the face of the blade angled slightly towards the hull and the whole paddle leaning outwards so that the upper grip is further out than the lower. The lower arm should be straight and the upper arm bent at the elbow. Pushing with the upper arm, pull the blade back in a shallow arc, initially towards the hull, allowing the blade to angle 'under' the canoe. As it passes your body, angle the face of the blade away from the hull. At the end of the stroke twist the blade through ninety degrees to feather it and push back in the wide arc on the surface of the water to the starting position. It is not necessary to lift the blade from the water. Repeat on the same side. If the canoe tends to turn away from the paddling side increase the curve of the arc at the

beginning of the stroke, i.e. pulling in a little more towards the hull at the beginning of the stroke and pushing away a little more at the end.

Because the canoe has more initial stability than the kayak it is possible to kneel nearer the side on which you are paddling, this will have the effect of making the canoe turn slightly towards this side thus assisting straight line paddling.

Paddling backwards

To paddle backwards, use the same stroke in reverse. It will take practice to learn this basic stroke. A similar, but slightly easier stroke, which can be used by the 'stern man' in a double canoe, is the J-stroke. This is a less efficient stroke than the basic one but may be found easier to learn initially.

The J-stroke

Begin, as before, with the blade placed in the water a comfortable distance ahead of the kneeling position with the face of the blade slightly angled towards the canoe. Pushing with the upper arm and pulling with the lower, draw the blade back, allowing it to angle 'under' the hull. As it passes the body position begin to twist the face of the blade away from the canoe and, at the same time, push it out, away from the hull. It should finish at an angle of about forty-five degrees and at this point will be acting as a rudder. Finally, at the end of the stroke, lever the blade outwards against the gunwale in a flick movement. With increased proficiency this levering can be lessened but without it the J-stroke is tiring. The recovery action is with the paddle almost flat above the gunwales and the blade describing a wide arc forwards to the starting position for the next stroke. The J-stroke is not possible using the bent shaft paddle. All the kayak strokes may be used in the canoe although the two support strokes are unlikely to be required by the tourist. The draw strokes are useful though, for they can be used not only for moving the canoe sideways but as an additional means of steering. Normal steering is as that for the kayak, i.e. by means of sweep strokes, forward and reverse, or by varying the basic forward paddling strokes. If you usually paddle on the left and are facing a right hand bend in a river it may be negotiated by simply paddling 'straight' on the left, i.e. without the curve to the stroke which is incorporated to enable the canoe to be kept straight. A bend to the left could entail increasing the curve to the stroke or perhaps changing paddling sides. This is quite permissible and is good practice from time to time since it allows a change of position and brings another set of muscles into use.

In all cases the faster the water is flowing the greater will be the effect on the paddle blade and the more rapidly will changes take place. This is true whether the flow is due to the speed of the craft through the water or simply to the speed of the river current.

The two-man canoe

So far we have been considering the solo paddler and this in the case of the kayak is perhaps best for, used solo, the kayak is a very manoeuvrable and satisfying craft. However, the canoe, paddled as a double, is perhaps even more manoevrable and can certainly be just as satisfactory for the crew. By combining strokes the crew can control their craft to a remarkable degree – the slalom C2 can even be rolled. Keeping straight is no problem and the basic steering is the concern of the stern man.

Because the canoe is narrow at the stern paddling position it is not necessary for the stern paddler to angle the paddle blade at the start of the J-stroke, nor is it usually necessary to touch the gunwale: the remainder of the stroke is as described for the solo paddler.

The normal bow stroke is a simple paddle stroke made parallel to the centre line of the canoe with a recovery arc similar to that described for the basic stroke in solo paddling, steering being the stern paddler's responsibility. However on a rapid river it may be advisable to allow the bow paddler to initiate the steering movements since he is nearer the action! In any event close co-operation is essential.

6

On the Water - More Advanced
Paddling Strokes

The paddling strokes described in Chapter 5 are adequate for
canoeing on lowland rivers, lakes and canals but in wilder water,
found on rapid rivers and the sea, other strokes will be required.
In general these are dynamic, like the slap support and draw, and
so cannot be performed half-heartedly or slowly if they are to be
successful. Such strokes are usually most effective when moving
fast, or in a rapid current. The hands remain in the normal
paddling position for each of these strokes. In some cases this
may feel strange at first but it is essential as it makes it possible
to change from one stroke to another in mid-move without hesita-
tion. I shall describe the strokes for the double bladed paddle but
since most, if not all, have been developed from the similar strokes
used by the single bladed canoe paddler they can all be performed
with the single blade, and may indeed be easier.

Stern rudder

The simplest method of turning is to place the paddle blade in the
water behind the seat position, with the back of the blade facing
forwards about 50 cm (20 in) away from the hull. The craft will
turn about the blade but slows rapidly thus reducing the stroke's
effectiveness. The turn may be tightened, and the whole move
made more interesting, by turning the blade into the sculling
position, i.e. leading edge of the blade angled upwards. Lean on

the blade and sweep it forwards, recovering as it passes forward of the seat position. This is a particularly useful stroke for controlling direction when surfing. In this case it can be used to enable the kayak to remain on a wave. If the blade is moved towards the stern, steering control is exerted in the opposite direction.

Low telemark

The *low telemark* is a turning stroke which may be developed from the stern rudder. The blade is placed in the water near the stern back down with the leading edge angled upwards. Lean on the blade and sweep it forwards, recovering as the blade passes the cockpit. Increased forward speed will permit more lean which will increase the rate of turn because if you can heel your craft until it is turning on the gunwale the effective waterline length is very much reduced. The effective rocker of the gunwale line is equal to half the beam, i.e. approximately 30 cm (12 in).

High telemark

The *high telemark* is closely related to the low and is performed similarly but with the *face* of the paddle blade facing forwards and down. The wrist nearest the working blade should be twisted down while the upper forearm is near the forehead. The paddle loom is therefore more upright than in the low telemark and the action is more of a hanging than a leaning move; the kayak, in trying to slide away from the blade, is held by it. The high telemark is used when breaking into, and out of, rapid water and this will be considered further in Chapter 7.

The high telemark lends itself to combination with other strokes and may be completed with a variation of the draw stroke to bring the bow into the turn, or possibly to stabilise the craft.

Hanging draw stroke

This leads us to the *hanging draw* stroke, the single bladed version of which is sometimes called the *stationary draw*. This is a method of moving the craft sideways rapidly without necessarily altering its direction. The blade is placed in the water beside or a little behind the seat position with the face of the blade towards the hull, about 50 cm (20 in) out, and the leading edge angled outwards. The blade must be held firmly in position with the upper hand near the forehead or higher. With the kayak moving fast lean on the blade. Recover when it is next to the hull. Twist your body sideways for this stroke and adjust the position of the blade and the angle until you can move your craft with predictable results. This is a useful support stroke in sea waves.

Draw turn

The *draw turn* is intended both to turn and move the craft sideways while it is moving forwards, or in a fast current. The paddle is held with the loom vertical, face of the blade towards the hull, but with its leading edge angled outward, and is placed in the water at the side of the cockpit while in this position. The craft will be drawn towards the blade and will turn around it. An obvious use for this stroke is in drawing the craft away from a bank, and turning it downstream, in a rapid river.

Bow rudder

Another effective steering stroke for the bow paddler in a canoe is the *bow rudder*. The craft must be moving at a reasonable speed for it, and the next stroke, to be fully effective. Put the blade, on its normal side, i.e. the right blade on the right hand side of the hull, in the water near the bow with the face of the blade towards the hull. The upper blade of the double paddle should be over the shoulder on the same side with the upper arm bent at the elbow while the lower arm is extended. Do not try this with too much speed for the initial attempts. Practise, as always, on both sides until proficient.

Cross-bow rudder

A little more difficult to perform, but an even more effective variation is the *cross-bow rudder*. Here the blade is placed in the water on the 'wrong' side of the hull, still with the face of the blade towards the hull. In making a right turn the left blade is put in the water on the right side of the bowl. The left arm is extended forwards while the right may be low, near the deck, or above shoulder level depending on whether you have the working blade shallow or deep. The deeper the blade and the faster your speed through the water the more effective the action – and the more effective the capsizing moment. Practise the action at slow speeds and work on both sides.

Ferry glide

As will have been realised by now each of these strokes requires a lot of practice if they are to be perfected. Suppleness around the waistline is a considerable help! Each stroke has been described without reference to current flow but this can have considerable effect and may actually determine which stroke is most practicable in any circumstance. (See Chapters 7 and 8 on river and sea techniques.) However, there is one situation where the current is essential if the manoeuvre is to be carried out – this is the *ferry glide*.

The name derives from the river ferries where the ferry boat is moored by means of a very long wire or chain stretching upstream

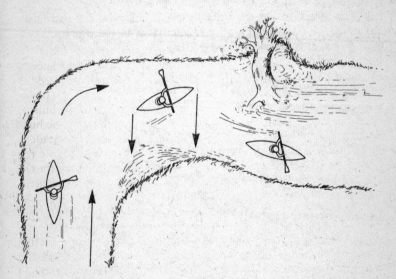

FIG. 6
The Ferry Glide. Utilised here to negotiate a fallen tree which is partially blocking the stream.

either to one bank of the river or to the centre of a chain across it. To cross, the ferry boat is given a sheer into the stream by means of a large rudder. The water pressure on the rudder moves the ferry across the river in an arc whose centre is at the point where the mooring line is fixed. The more rapid the river current the more effective is the ferry, and of course, the less likely it would be to have a normal motorised ferry.

In a canoe or kayak this can be utilised to move from one side of a river to the other to survey the best course past some obstruction. Because the canoe is not moored it is necessary to paddle, either forwards or backwards, in order to stay in the same place relative to the bank. Check that you are able to do this against the current before it is too late to retreat to the bank. Assuming you are travelling downstream, back paddle until you are stationary relative to the bank. Now angle the stern of your craft towards the bank you wish to approach and the pressure of the water on the hull will move you across the river in this direction. It is essential, of course, to continue back paddling sufficiently to maintain your relative position. To change direction swing your craft to angle in the opposite direction. In the unlikely event that you are travelling upstream the bow is angled into the current in the direction you wish to travel to obtain the same effect.

7

On the River

One of the joys of canoeing is discovering that no two rivers are the same, and that it is possible for the character of a river to change within hours. This makes it difficult to categorise rivers other than in broad terms. In Britain rivers may be thought of as lowland and tamed, or rapid and untamed. For the most part those in the south are tamed while those running through mountainous and moorland areas are untamed. Each river changes its character during the course of its path to the sea. Short term changes must be anticipated on rivers fed from mountainous areas, for rain falling on hills very quickly finds its way into feeder streams and tributaries. Such rivers may rise several feet in an extremely short period of time, so this is something to be considered when choosing a camp site near a mountain fed river too.

Lowland rivers which may be navigated by all kinds of craft do not warrant any form of descriptive grading as they are entirely predictable, except possibly in times of spate.

White water grades

Rapid or white water rivers are graded from 1–6. Grade 1 is an 'easy' river with occasional small rapids where care may be required to negotiate obstacles, both natural and man-made. Grade 2 is 'medium' where rapids are more frequent but the course taken remains reasonably easy to recognise. Grade 3 is 'difficult', the course will not always be easy to pick out and rapids will be numerous with irregular waves, broken water, eddies and whirlpools. Grade 4, 'very difficult', is similar to Grade 3 – but more so – and may warrant inspection from the bank; Grade 5, 'exceedingly difficult' is self-explanatory, and Grade 6 is 'the absolute limit of difficulty' and may only be attempted with some risk to life.

With the advent of the GRP canoe, and the consequent development of skills and abilities, many rivers have in effect been downgraded to bring them into line with modern expectations. Some rivers will have a dual grading in an attempt to grade variations more accurately. In venturing on to rapid rivers the newcomer must use common sense and take care not to exceed his own capabilities. Experience can only be gained by venturing further, but take care and do it safely.

White water rivers are not usually worth canoeing until they have matured a little, and as most will require permission for canoeing, you will be able to discover the best starting point at the same time. Similarly, if it is white water in which you are interested – and why else would you be on the river at all? – it will probably not be worthwhile remaining on the river for its full length below the starting point, although an interesting estuary can provide excellent canoeing.

'Tamed' rivers

Many canoeists begin their canoeing activities on lowland rivers, so let us consider some of the possible 'problems' the 'tamed' rivers give the beginner.

Locks and weirs

First are the locks and their (usually adjacent) weirs. The weir is simply a wall across the river to retain a certain head of water on the upstream side. When this level is exceeded, water flows over the weir into the lower section of the river. Normally there are sluices in the weir wall or in the bank which may be opened or closed to control the flow in times of drought or flood. In this way the level of one section of river can be lowered to maintain the flow in a lower section; conversely the sluices may also be opened to allow flood water to escape down the river rather than breaking the banks. If the river is controlled by a weir it then becomes necessary to provide some means of getting craft past the weir and this is done by means of locks.

Locks enable craft to by-pass the weirs and at the same time allow them to be raised or lowered from one level of the river to another. They vary in construction but all are more or less rectangular basins, generally made of stone, brick or concrete with a gate (or gates) at each end, and a means of being emptied and filled. The most common has a pair of wooden gates at each end, so arranged that each pair forms a shallow V facing the upper level; thus the pressure of the water on the gates maintains them in the closed position. Some locks have only a single gate which bears against one side of the lock structure when closed; others have the lower gates replaced by a single steel gate which may swing up in an arc or be lifted vertically like a guillotine to allow craft to pass beneath.

Sluices (or 'slackers') are fitted either to the gates themselves or in the lock walls for filling and emptying. Where the single steel gate is fitted this may simply be wound open a little to empty the lock instead of having sluices.

Whatever the construction, the procedure for using locks remains the same.

Let us assume you are travelling downstream since this is the normal direction for the canoeist. You arrive at the lock, disembark and leave your craft securely moored. There is no point in lifting out if you are using the lock since if you carry out why not carry round and re-embark on the lower side? We find the lock full of water, the last user having travelled from the lower to the upper level. First check that the upper level sluices are closed. This is essential otherwise when you open the lower sluices to empty the lock the water will continue to flow into the lock from the upper level and in a canal this could seriously lower the level in the upper section or 'pound'. With upper sluices firmly closed you can open the upper gates, or just one perhaps for a canoe. Paddle in, or use the painters, to manoeuvre your craft into position. Somewhere in the middle is a good place to be, well clear of any other craft, especially large ones, for if they are badly handled they could easily crush the canoe in the turbulence which may occur when the lock is emptied or filled.

Occasionally there are ledges at the upper end of locks which are only visible when the lock is empty. If the upper gates are old with gaps where they should meet, large jets of water will spurt through –

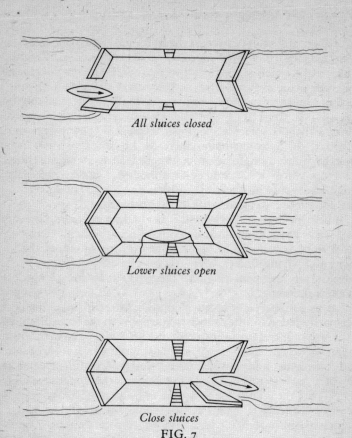

All sluices closed

Lower sluices open

Close sluices

FIG. 7

Negotiating a river or canal lock. Shows a canoe travelling downstream.

two good reasons for staying clear of the upper ends of locks! Tie your canoe in position if you are alone and close the upper gates. They may be reluctant to close fully, but don't worry for the water pressure you are about to release on them will complete the job. Walk to the lower end and open the sluices a little until you have a good flow of water leaving the lock. Return to your craft and control its descent into the lock with the painters. When the water level inside is the same as that at the lower level tie up again and close the lower sluices. (It is courtesy to close them for whoever follows you will have to do so in order to get through the lock.) Open the gate, line your canoe out into the lower level and paddle along to the next lock.

A companion avoids the need for tying up and lowering on the painters for there are usually ladders or chains set into the sides of the locks which provide hand holds for one canoeist who can control the two craft while the other manipulates the sluices and gates.

If you are travelling upstream, say on a canal, the procedure is reversed but do take care when filling the lock. Open the sluices a little at a time or the resulting turbulence could damage your canoe. Always leave the sluices closed unless other instructions are given at the lock.

Close contact with weirs should be avoided unless you have enough experience to make a reasonable assessment of the danger involved in 'shooting' the weir. Where a river is no longer generally navigable, its weirs may be broken, or in a poor state of repair. The hazards facing the canoeist may then include broken ironwork and masonry as well as the more obvious rough water. When in doubt, investigate closely and if you are still not sure carry around. There is little likelihood of being inadvertently swept over a weir because, unless you intend to shoot it, there is no reason for going close. You will usually hear it in plenty of time to take avoiding action even if its position is not at first clear. Broken and disused locks present similar problems and should be dealt with in the same way.

Other hazards

Other hazards may be natural – fallen trees or perhaps rocks – or man-made, and here the list is almost inexhaustible. While paddling down what appears to be a pleasant stream, miles from human influence, you are quite likely to be faced with barbed wire, old beds, rusty bicycles, and anything else your fellow man no longer requires.

Bridges

Also man-made, but encountered more frequently, are bridges. These present no unusual problems in normal conditions. If you are canoeing a rapid river you will expect the current to become even more rapid where it is constricted by the piers of a bridge. The same effect may be less obvious on a larger, apparently placid, river but it is still present. As a beginner, approach bridges with care, it is always possible that maintenance or repairs are being carried out so be prepared to ferry glide from one arch to another and do not underestimate the pressure of the current.

In times of spate all hazards, even apparently minor ones, are prospective accident sites and should be approached with extra care since a relatively insignificant incident can result in a fatality. One such example occurred when a canoeist became jammed in his kayak. The river was in spate and the water was cold, as a result the canoeist became exhausted, and with water breaking over him he died as rescuers were trying in vain to free him. I mention this for although fatalities are rare in canoeing they can result from one small incident which goes 'wrong'. Other factors intrude and, before you are able to prevent it, the whole thing is out of hand. Accidents, are more often than not preventable with forethought and care. There is no substitute for experience but this must be acquired sensibly. This is of particular importance should you find yourself in a position where you are responsible for the well-being and safety of others.

River flow

So far we have been considering what might be thought of as the extraneous factors on the river – locks, weirs, bridges – but there is the natural path of the water to be considered too. Anything which affects the flow of water can have its effect on a small craft and must be understood by the canoeist if he is to make the most of the river on which he is travelling.

Generally the caneoist will want to follow the path of the main flow of the river, this will offer the deepest water and the fastest current flow – the outside of bends is an example. However, rivers of interest to canoeists are usually rather more complex and will offer conditions of considerable variation. The 'tamed' river will be of a fairly constant depth because it is controlled by the weirs, thus the river bed will have little effect on the water.

Rapids

This is not so on a rapid river and as the water depth is reduced the shape and condition of the river bed will have an increasing effect;

fast water flowing shallow over a rock strewn bed will produce a lot of haphazard waves which are loosely referred to as 'rapids'. As the water depth and current increase the waves become larger until the point is reached where the river bed is sufficiently far from the surface for the resulting disturbance of the water to hardly show. If the depth increases further the surface flow will become smooth while remaining fast. Obviously if the rocks on the river bed are large their effect will be felt, and seen, through a larger range of water depths. The speed of the current will also have its effect – the faster the flow the bigger the waves formed when the water is diverted by rocks.

Eddies

Large rocks and boulders may protrude above the surface of the river. According to the grading of the river the path the canoeist takes may be obvious, but remember, where the river is constricted in this way the current will increase in speed. Below the obstruction some water will flow in behind giving a current flow contrary to that on each side of it. This contrary flow is called an *eddy*. Canoeists can use eddies, (which may also occur in other situations, on the inside of bends for example), as a means of working up against the prevailing current, when breaking out of rapids, and, in fact, whenever such a contrary flow may help him. Learn to recognise where eddies are likely to occur, and try to pick them out from the main flow of the current. Floating objects, such as small branches, leaves and twigs, often are temporarily trapped in them and are good indicators of current flow. An eddy can develop into a whirlpool but the beginner is unlikely to meet these until he ventures on to the more extreme rivers, and by this time he should have gained sufficient experience to be able to deal with it!

'Stoppers'

When fast-flowing, shallow water runs on to a deeper and slower flowing section of the river a series of standing waves are formed by the faster water bouncing back from the deeper layer of slower water. The first of these waves can be quite large, depending upon the current flow, and is known as a *stopper* because the water in it forms a vertical eddy and is actually flowing back *upstream*. To get through a stopper of any size you must paddle hard to overcome the contrary flow of the water. Below the stopper will usually be a series

of smaller, standing waves sometimes referred to as 'haystacks'.
These do not have the power of the stopper and may offer a good
opportunity for practising white water techniques. This type of
river condition may be experienced below weirs when the sluices
are opened in times of spate. Some of the Thames weirs are quite
good examples.

Horizontal eddies usually offer a chance of approaching the
waves – but be prepared for a capsize! The usual long stopper wave
below the weir should be avoided for it is possible to become trapped
between the wave and the weir itself. This is an unenviable position
to be in and can be frightening if the stopper is of any size. It may
also be very difficult to escape from. If you should find yourself
trapped like this the easiest way out is at the ends providing there is
no retaining wall. Where there is a wall at both ends it may just be
possible to do a high draw stroke over the stopper so that the paddle
blade enters the downstream flowing water. This will pull you over
the stopper – but only if it is fairly small. Failing this it may be
necessary to abandon your canoe. In this case there are two
alternatives. Either climb out on to the weir sill itself and walk to the
end or jump over the stopper into the water below; or if you capsize
between the stopper and weir, swim out *under* the stopper. You may
need to take your life-jacket off and so *this should only be considered
as a last resort*. Informed opinion states that in these circumstances
it may be better to keep your life-jacket on and relax until the water
ejects you below the stopper in its own good time. The choice is
yours and all in all weir stoppers are not for the inexperienced.

Going with the current

As far as is possible the canoeist should go with the current when
manoeuvering. A simple example of this is leaving the river bank on
embarkation. Assuming the canoe is facing upstream with the bank
on the right all that is necessary to turn into the stream is a left bow
rudder stroke. This will pull the bow into the stream. Then lean
downstream, and continue the turn with a paddle stroke on the
right. With increased current flow it may be better to make the
initial move with a draw turn.

The lean *downstream* is an essential of river turns for if you lean
upstream the water on the deck is very likely to capsize you.
Remember, when breaking out of the fast flowing mainstream

current into an eddy, that you will be dealing with counter flowing current – lean downstream in the eddy as you leave the mainstream – nice timing is called for.

8

Sea Canoeing

Sea canoeing represents, perhaps, the greatest challenge to the canoeist. But even if you never venture out of sight of land the sea can offer a new dimension to your canoeing. It cannot be over-emphasised however that the sea is not to be considered lightly. No canoeist should leave shore with less than two companions. If he does he is gambling with his life. Three experienced canoeists should be able to help themselves in reasonable conditions. In unreasonable conditions they may well drown.

Waves

The sea is infinitely variable. It is never still, it is affected by the moon, the wind, the sun, the depth of water, and the distance from land. The most obvious movement is that of the waves which are created by the wind. In areas where the wind has a large distance over which it can create waves (fetch) they may build up to considerable heights – the Southern Ocean is an example of such an area. The resulting height of a wave will depend upon the strength of the wind creating it, the length of time that wind has been blowing, the distance over which it has blown, and the depth of the water.

Also of interest to the canoeist is the movement of the water within the wave. If a cross-section is taken through a wave formation (Fig. 8) it will be seen that there is a *wave length* taken between the crests of a pair of waves, and *wave height* or *amplitude* measured from the bottom of the trough to the crest. Within an individual wave the water particles are rotating in a roughly circular orbit in the same direction as the wave is moving. This orbit is not subject to the same vertical movement as the wave, thus while the water particle movement on the face of the wave is downwards just below the crest, it is *backwards* in the trough and on the back of the wave. This water particle movement explains why, when a wave

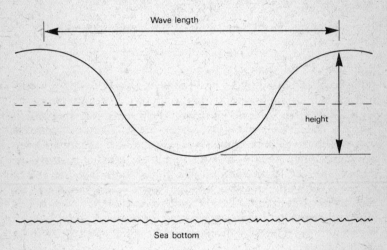

FIG. 8
Cross-section through a wave formation showing wave length and height or amplitude.

reaches shallow water it, in effect, trips itself on the bottom and breaks. The sea does not need to be shallow before waves will break. A wave breaks when it begins to 'feel' the bottom and this will occur when the depth of the water is less than half the wave length, or one and one half times the wave height. In deep water a wave may break, too, when its height becomes larger than one-seventh of its wave length – although this is academic for our purposes. Of more immediate interest are the waves one is most likely to encounter on beaches. These, like the sea itself, are infinitely variable but do fall between two clearly defined types.

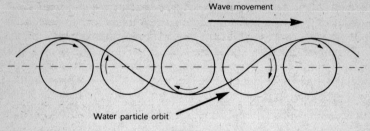

Wave movement

Water particle orbit

FIG. 9

Illustrates the water particle movement in wave formation.

Surf waves and 'dumpers'

If the beach slopes gently towards the deeper water waves will break
as they reach the shallows and in the right conditions *surf waves* will
form. Where the beach slopes steeply the waves do not break until
they are almost on the beach and the break is very sudden and
violent. This type of breaking wave is known as a *dumper*. Beaches
on which dumpers are breaking should be avoided, if possible,
particularly for landing for if you allow yourself to be swung
broadside on to the breaking waves you could find yourself being
turned over and over against the beach as successive waves break.
The undertow from such beaches is strong, too, for the volume of
water in each wave has to escape very rapidly below the next
breaking wave.

Getting afloat

Getting afloat from a beach is not difficult except where the beach is
steep and dumpers are breaking. The easiest method is to have the
kayak just afloat, pointing out to sea. Choose your moment between
waves, get in and fasten your spray cover. Do not allow your paddle
to float away. When the next wave swirls around you, push your
hands down on the beach at each side of the cockpit and ease
yourself into deeper water. As soon as the stern is clear of the beach,
paddle through the incoming waves until clear of any which are
breaking. If you have short arms use a hand on one side of the kayak
and a paddle held vertically on the other to push yourself of. You
must keep paddling through the waves for, if you stop as a wave hits

you, you will probably swing broadside on and capsize. If there is no convenient beach it really becomes a matter of experience and knowing your own capabilities when it comes to boarding.

Coming ashore

Coming ashore is equally simple – on a reasonably gently sloping beach try to ride a wave until it leaves you aground, then get out quickly and carry your kayak above the water level. Landing on a dumper beach is more difficult and the technique used depends upon the steepness of the beach. It may be possible to approach normally and if you pick your wave well there will be just seconds to get free of your kayak before being swept away by the next wave.

If the beach is very steep this method may be inadvisable because of the possiblity of nose-diving into the beach with the likelihood of serious damage to you and your kayak. In this case, if landing is essential at this particular point, swing broadside on to the beach at the last possible moment and, again, get out very quickly. Help from onshore can be most useful in these circumstances. It is also possible, in some instances, to let yourself be swept on to the beach broadside on while riding a wave, judicious control being exerted by means of stern rudder or hanging draw strokes.

The wind

The effect of wind has already been mentioned but in addition to its role in creating waves the wind can also modify their shape. As wind speed decreases the waves created by it decrease in height but their speed and length remain the same. This *swell* can persist many miles from the source of the original waves and may then have 'local' waves imposed upon it. The Atlantic coast of Britain is rarely, if ever, free of the Atlantic swell generated many miles away by unseen storms. If a local wind blows on this swell in the same direction, surf waves will build up on the *lee shore* towards which the wind and the swell are moving. If the wind is blowing in opposition to the swell, short, steep waves will form and may break making for difficult canoeing. If you are paddling away from a *windward shore* (that is with the wind behind you) towards a lee shore, you must expect the sea to become rougher as you get further offshore.

Problems of paddling at sea

Paddling in swell usually presents few problems for the crests will be flattened, the effect being like paddling across undulations. With the wind against the waves, paddling is less easy and maintaining a specific course may be difficult without a rudder or a straight keeled sea kayak.

The problems of paddling a kayak at sea are related to the size of the waves, both in their height and length. Because of the rotary movement of the water particles in the waves the kayak will be accelerated forwards on the crests and decelerated in the troughs when paddling in the direction in which the waves are moving. The opposite is true when paddling into the waves. When paddling at an angle other than ninety degrees to the waves it is necessary to compensate for this water movement as paddling at an angle to the waves but in the same direction as they are moving results in the bow of the kayak being swung first towards the waves then, as the crest passes under the canoe, it will swing the bows away from the waves. This directional instability is soon appreciated and if much sea canoeing is contemplated a properly designed sea kayak should be considered essential.

Paddling parallel to the waves raises the question of lateral stability. This is most likely to be noticeable on the wave crests where you are most exposed to the wind. The troughs are less of a problem. Again, because of the water particle movement you should lean *into* the waves both as they approach and as they recede. With practice a rhythm develops and you are able to concentrate on achieving your course. On a breaking wave it will be necessary to make a conscious effort to remain upright by using one of the dynamic support strokes.

Tides

In addition to the effect of the wind it is necessary to take into account the effect of the tide. In general, the wind will be blowing in the same direction as the waves since it has created them. (An exception is where a local wind has superimposed waves on an existing swell.) This means that if the tide is flowing in opposition to the wind – and consequent waves – the effective wave length will be shortened and the height or amplitude will be increased. Where there is a strong tidal stream, this can produce very high and dangerous waves. Local knowledge may well be necessary to ascertain where such conditions are likely to occur and at what state of the tide. (Tides and their effects are considered in further detail in the next chapter.)

Precautions for canoeing at sea

As I write this it is a beautiful spring day with the sun blazing from a cloudless sky and the Thames Estuary off the North Kent Coast like a mill pond. On days such as this sea canoeing appears about as hazardous as a trip on a canal, and perhaps, if all you propose is a paddle of a few miles along the coast, there will be no problems. However, with sea canoeing do be prepared for the worst. Listen to the weather forecast for the period you expect to be afloat; know what the tide is going to be doing in your area during the same period; familiarise yourself with any local peculiarities when the tide changes. These are just some of the external factors affecting the safety of the canoeist at sea.

At a more personal level you should have at least two companions as two competent and practised canoeists can rescue a third even if his canoe is swamped. It will not sink of course because of its fixed-in buoyancy. Sea canoeists disagree on the necessity of carrying a chart. In my opinion it is better to have a sketch and notes of your route to hand, and leave the chart in a waterproof bag inside the kayak. This is discussed in detail in the next chapter.

A compass is essential for the sea canoeist, if only as an aid to recognising the chosen landmarks of your course. Weather conditions on the coast – and even more so at sea – can change very rapidly. Heat haze or sea mist can reduce visibility drastically in minutes and disorientation can follow quickly. It is in such conditions that a compass can become a very comforting piece of equipment, but is only of use if you know in which direction to paddle to reach the shore or your destination.

It is assumed that your sea kayak is properly equipped with deck lines, buoyancy, a properly fitting spray cover, and possibly a bilge pump for emptying the cockpit in the event of a swamping. A spare paddle (of the type which is in two sections with a ferruled joint) should be carried on the deck.

Paddles for sea canoeing can, with advantage, be a little longer than those used inland. The length should be added to the blade which may then be narrower to give the same area. In use the paddle should be held lower so the blade bites less deeply into the water – in effect 'low gear' paddling, which also aids steering. A back support may also be found helpful but do not be tempted to lean backwards for this is both inefficient and tiring.

Sea sickness medicine may be required, but this is something you will discover only by experience. Sea sickness is very debilitating and in cold conditions can accelerate the onset of hypothermia and should be prevented for this reason if for no other. If the proposed trip is more than a short one, food should be carried. This must obviously be accessible – snack foods, such as sweet bars, can be carried in a pouch pocket on the life-jacket cover, while hot drinks and soup and more bulky, but easily assimilated foods, can be carried in the watertight compartment in the sea kayak where they can easily be retrieved by a companion. In the normal kayak it is usually possible to store small items next to or just behind the seat. This does mean having to remove at least part of your spray cover to gain access but this should be safe enough in a *raft*.

The raft is formed when two or more canoeists come together with their paddles across the decks of their kayaks so each paddler can hold both the loom of his own paddle and that of his neighbour. If a tighter formation is required, hold onto the coamings. The facing direction of the raft can be controlled to some extent by the end paddlers but it will drift, probably with the wind rather than the tide, depending upon the relative strength of each.

Sea rescues

Once you are at sea, you and your companions are very much on your own. The experience of shipwrecked yachtsmen suggest that the chances of being seen and rescued in an emergency at sea are not good even if you fire flares when a potential rescuer is sighted. Since an orange, inflated life raft is likely to be more visible than a kayak this suggests that self-sufficiency is the only aim for the sea canoeist. Flares and/or smoke making devices are expensive but should be carried since in an emergency every step towards recovery and safety should be anticipated and the means of achieving it should be available when required. The sea canoeist is usually in a slightly better situation than the shipwrecked yachtsman since he should have informed the local coast-guard of his intentions and should also have someone ashore who will alert the emergency service if his group does not report back by a specified time. The group should also be in a reasonably restricted area where the search can be concentrated. A radio tranceiver is another possible safety aid which could be considered, although the small VHF sets currently available have a limited range and a GPO licence is required for their operation. A small radio receiver is useful for longer trips if it can pick up the shipping weather forecasts on the long waveband.

However, self-sufficiency must be the aim of the sea canoeist and it must be accepted that contrary to other sea going craft the kayak will not look after its crew if he becomes exhausted or otherwise incapable. The raft may offer some respite but even this relies on the canoeists to maintain it, regardless of the prevailing conditions.

The ability to roll your kayak upright in the event of a capsize is essential. I am not convinced that it is possible to teach yourself to roll from written instructions – although there have been some good attempts – so, apart from suggesting that you enrol for a course of rolling lessons, I do not propose going further into this aspect of canoeing. The whole point of rolling is that it brings the canoeist upright without leaving the kayak.

The same result can be achieved by means of an *Eskimo rescue*. It is essential that spray covers are a good tight fit on the cockpit rim for this rescue. A member of the group capsizes and dog-paddles on one side of his kayak to keep his head above water. The rescuer quickly positions his kayak alongside that of the victim and places his paddle across the bottom of the capsized kayak and on his own cockpit. The victim then places his hands on the paddle loom and so rights himself by pulling up on it. The two kayaks ramain rafted together until the victim is in a satisfactory condition to continue. An alternative approach is to have the rescuer nose the bow of his kayak into reach of the victim's hands who then pulls up on the bow. The disadvantages of this method are the danger of hitting the victim on the head which is highly likely in any kind of a sea; the fact that the rescuer is not in physical contact with the victim; and finally the rescuer is less stable.

If the victim bales out, or the spray cover is released, before an Eskimo rescue can be effected, all is not lost. You can attempt a *deep water rescue*. Several methods have been devised but the two I shall describe are, in my opinion, the most practical.

It is vital that the victim be reassured and replaced in his kayak as quickly as possible for, even in summer, the water temperature around our coasts is low enough to cause rapid hypothermia in a wet and possibly frightened canoeist. Fear can accelerate the effect of cold water so it is back into the kayak or, if the capsize is within the breakers just offshore, you can accompany the victim back to shore while he swims with his kayak. An assisted rescue in the breaker area is virtually impossible.

The three essentials of any rescue operation are:

1 Emptying and righting the kayak;
2 Getting the victim back into his kayak in the shortest possible time;
3 The whole operation being capable of successful performance in calm or rough water conditions.

The 'HI' rescue

The method known as the 'HI' meets these criteria most closely in my experience. Two rescue kayaks are required. The victim leaves his kayak inverted and holds on to his own paddle and the toggle or deck-line at the *end* of his kayak. It is essential that he does not try to hang on at the centre because the combination of his weight scrabbling about at this position and the waves will turn his kayak upright filling it with water and making the rescue more difficult. The two rescue kayaks raft up on the inverted kayak, one on each side. It does not matter if they are facing in opposite directions – in fact it is an advantage in some ways if they are. They place their two paddles across their own cockpits, in front of themselves, and across the bottom of the inverted kayak. The victim must now transfer his hold to the end of one of the rescue kayaks, retaining his grasp of one kayak at all times – and this is one of the advantages of having the rescuers facing in opposite directions, as the victim is in view at all times.

Slide the inverted kayak under the paddles and lift the end nearest the victim on to the paddle looms. Ensure that the kayak remains inverted. Using the deck lines, slide it over the looms until it is positioned with its cockpit over the paddles. The victim can now pull down on the end of the kayak which will enable the water at the other end to run from the cockpit. When that end is empty rock the kayak back to drain the remaining water and right it while on the paddle looms. Slide it back into the water under the looms. Re-entry can now be made between two of the kayaks while they are held in a raft by the rescuers. The victim lies back in the water with his hands and forearms over the decks of the kayaks (one of which is his own). He then lets his feet and legs float upwards and lifts them into the cockpit of his own kayak. It is then a relatively easy matter for him to slide into the cockpit, assisted if need be by the rescuers. It does not matter if he is facing the wrong way for it is an easy move for him to get his bottom on to the deck of his kayak and then turn into the correct position – the object is to get the victim out of the water as quickly as possible.

Re-entry may also be made across the front deck of one of the rescuing kayaks but I am not sure that this method is any easier for the victim or the rescuers and it must be borne in mind that the rescuers may be required to perform several rescues if a group of inexperienced canoeists are involved.

In theory the 'HI' method of deep water rescue can be used where the kayak has become filled with water, but in my experience this requires very strong rescuers and kayaks to withstand the considerable weight which will be imposed on the foredecks. This reinforces the necessity for all sea going kayaks to be almost completely filled with buoyancy material below decks or to have water-tight bulkheads each side of the cockpit and a pump for emptying the cockpit area.

The 'X' Rescue

It is possible to perform a deep water rescue with only one rescuing kayak using the 'X' rescue method. Again the victim leaves his kayak inverted. The rescuer grasps the kayak by the toggle or deckline at one end and lifts this end on to his own foredeck. Using a steady pull he then pulls it across the deck until the cockpit is on his foredeck. The victim has now positioned himself on the side towards which his kayak is being pulled so he can reach up and pull down the end thus allowing the water to drain from the lower end. The inverted kayak can now be righted, replaced in the water and re-entry made. This method is harder on the rescuer than the 'HI' and depends, too, upon having kayaks with strong foredecks. (It reinforces the rule which says that canoeists venturing on to the sea should not do so in groups of less than three.) Re-entry is most easily made across the empty kayak since this acts as a float to help stabilise the rescuing craft.

Where sea kayaks, which have sealed cockpit areas and a bilge pump for emptying, are being used the rescue is much easier since all that is necessary is for the victim to be replaced in his kayak which he can then empty himself while in a raft.

If the original capsize was due to an inability to cope with the prevailing conditions it is highly likely that further capsizes will occur and the expedition should end immediately. In cold conditions, even when suitably clothed, the number of rescues which can be accomplished before the rescuers are exhausted is limited. This is yet another factor which must be considered when deciding whether or not to proceed with a proposed sea journey by kayak.

Safety boats

Mention should perhaps be made of safety boats. I am not sure that safety boats are very much use except when it is necessary to remove fatigued paddlers from the water. This could occur for example, crossing the English Channel in good weather. Where paddlers cannot cope with the sea it is likely to be extremely hazardous to try to transfer to a safety boat unless this is a large inflatable handled by a very competent crew, and even then injuries may be caused.

Quite recently, during the summer, a group of canoeists, apparently well equipped, set out from Folkstone to paddle to Dover Harbour. They had a motor boat accompanying them. The weather deteriorated and by the time they had reached the western entrance to the harbour it was too bad for me to consider taking a group of youngsters out *in* the harbour. There was apparently a problem with commercial traffic in the entrance and most of the canoeists were unable to get into the harbour through the western entrance. They paddled on, with the intention of making their entry at the eastern end. The alarm was raised which involved calling out the Dover lifeboat and the RAF rescue helicopter. The canoeists were all rescued – some from an area well east of the harbour where they had been swept by wind and sea. The motor boat was apparently unable to offer much assistance. I recount this episode without comment but as an example of a short sea trip which could have gone most terribly wrong.

The sea canoeist *must* aim at sensible self-sufficiency once he has taken the decision to venture on to the sea. Finally, it is worth mentioning that sea canoeing is now becoming organised with the forming of the Advanced Sea Kayak Club and the grading of coastal waters to give some indication of the degree of difficulty which may be expected.

9

Coastal Canoeing

The canoeist venturing on to the sea around our coasts also has to contend with all the other users of the sea. He owes it to himself and them to be aware of the rules governing the use of the sea in the same way as the cyclist must know and obey the road traffic laws. *The Seaway Code,* prepared by the Department of Trade and the Central Office of Information, can be obtained from the coastguard, Marine Survey Offices, or direct from the Department of Trade, Room 306, Gaywood House, Great Peter Street, London, SW1P 3LW. Fortunately in Great Britain we have remarkably free use of the sea around our coasts in that small private craft do not have to be registered or report their travel, unless returning from abroad. Long may this freedom continue, but it is quite possibly subject to continued sensible use of the sea by the private boat owner, including of course the canoeist.

In Chapter 8 I dealt, in a general way, with the handling of a kayak on the sea. I now propose to consider more specifically the practicalities of canoeing from place to place on the coast. Coastal navigation is perhaps a rather grand term for the sea travelling canoeist but is necessary for any craft making coastal voyages.

Equipment

The equipment required for making a coastal passage by canoe is not extensive. It is assumed that you will normally be in visual contact with the coast except for relatively short periods – when crossing an estuary, for example. Most important is a reliable compass. This should be capable of being read accurately on a very mobile kayak; a cheap type with a needle or card which spins at the slightest provocation will be next to useless. There is some case for having one which may be used in the hand for taking bearings but this is not essential. An accurate, waterproof watch will also be necessary.

You will also need a chart, or charts, to cover the area of your proposed travels. Admiralty charts are probably most common but are large and flat or folded and this may be a disadvantage for the canoeist. Stanford charts are more colourful, tend to give information in a more simple way and are supplied folded. It is really a question of personal preference. Whichever type you use it will be necessary to learn the meanings of at least some of the symbols. The Admiralty chart No. 5011, is a booklet entitled *Symbols and Abbreviations used on Admiralty Charts* and gives necessary information. Do check that any chart you buy is the latest edition – there is no excuse for buying out-of-date editions of Admiralty charts for the agent can exchange them for the latest. However, even the latest edition may be made out of date by temporary or unforeseen contingencies, e.g. a recent wreck. Many of these are unlikely to affect the canoeist and you can update your own charts from *Notices to Mariners* which are obtainable from chart agents. Extracts are also published in yachting magazines which can often be seen in local public libraries.

It is possible to seal charts with adhesive plastics coatings, some of which are designed to allow writing on them. It's up to you to decide how to make best use of and preserve your charts – and they are worth preserving for they are an expensive item for the navigator these days.

Scale on the chart is taken from the latitude scales which are those at the *sides* of the chart NOT the top and bottom. One minute on the latitude scale is equal to one nautical mile which is 1853 metres (6080 feet).

Depths on the latest Admiralty charts are in metres and tenths of metres with the land heights given to the nearest metre. Earlier editions gave soundings in fathoms (6 feet) and feet with land heights in feet only. The 'metric' charts are clearly marked as such and use more colour than previous editions.

Chart datum is a fixed level taken on modern charts as the lowest astronomical tide which is the lowest level of the sea likely to occur. The level is most unlikely ever to fall below chart datum, thus the soundings will tend to err on the safe side so far as the navigator is concerned. (*Soundings* are depths below chart datum.)

Of particular interest to canoeists are *drying heights*; if an area of the sea bed will become exposed when the sea level falls to chart datum then the height *above* chart datum is expressed as a drying height. On the metric Admiralty charts these areas are shaded in green and, to distinguish drying heights from soundings, the former figures are underlined on the chart.

You will also find on Admiralty charts at various strategic points small diamonds with letters in them. Elsewhere on the chart will be found a table headed by the diamonds and the appropriate latitude and longitude. In a column below each is the *rate* (speed) and *set* (direction) of the tidal stream at that position for various times before and after high water at a local major port. Two rates are given, for spring tides and neap tides. Thus it is possible to get a reasonable idea of the direction and speed of the tidal stream for any time of the day and on any day of the year asuming that you also have tide tables for the same major port to enable you to determine whether the tides are spring or neap on the day in question.

Also available are tidal stream atlases, eleven of which cover the coasts around the UK, but these are by no means essential for the canoeist. Tidal stream charts are also included in Reed's *Nautical Almanac,* and on Stanford charts the tidal stream is shown for the area covered by the chart.

If you plot direct on to your chart remember to use only a soft pencil and very lightly, so the marks may be erased without damaging the chart. Old plots merely confuse the chart and make new work more difficult.

A parallel rule is useful for transferring position lines and taking off angles from the compass rose on the chart. A navigational protractor can also pay for itself, and a pair of dividers or good pencil compasses are essential for determining distances from the scale.

The canoeist will also find the appropriate O.S. maps useful for he will want to know where roads approach the sea for access, where the 'local' is, a post office perhaps and the multitude of other information easily obtained from the 50,000 Series O.S. maps.

While the canoeist is not usually very concerned about depths of water in general, he is interested in areas which dry out – and this may be a very optimistic term in some estuaries where the 'dry' areas may well be deep mud – but the chart symbols will keep you informed of this. A knowledge of how to determine the depth of water to be expected at any given state of the tide is simple. In very rough terms there are two high water points travelling around the earth so that any individual place will have two high water periods at roughly twelve hour intervals. Similarly there will be two low water periods in between at the same intervals. The difference between high and low water in one period is known as the *range* of the tide. When the effects of the sun and the moon are cumulative there will be particularly high and low tides, i.e. the range is large, these are *spring tides* and they occur just after the full and new moon.

When the effects of the sun and the moon are in opposition the range of the tides will be small with low high tides and high low tides, these are *neap tides*. Obviously there are two spring and two neap tides each month with all the other tides falling between these two extremes. This is by no means the full story but is sufficient for our present requirements.

You will see from your chart or tidal stream atlas that spring tides, not unexpectedly, give stronger streams than neap tides. If there were no tides the sea would take up what is called *mean sea level*. When the tide is rising it is said to be *flooding*, and when it is falling it is *ebbing*.

Tidal predictions are published in Reed's *Nautical Almanac* and in local tide tables (and often in local coastal newspapers) – do check whether times are given as Greenwich Mean Time (GMT) (– our 'winter' time – as in Reed's or adjusted for British Summer Time (BST).

A simple way of calculating the approximate height of a tide at any given point is by the *Rule of Twelfths*. This states that the tide rises or falls during its six hours as follows:

in the first hour	1/12 of the range
in the second hour	2/12 of the range
in the third hour	3/12 of the range
in the fourth hour	3/12 of the range
in the fifth hour	2/12 of the range
in the sixth hour	1/12 of the range

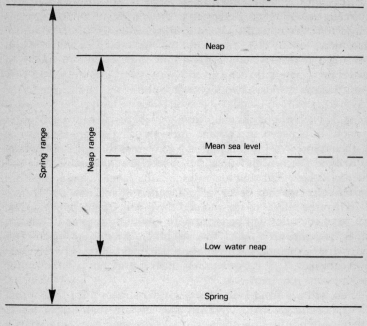

FIG. 10

The relationship between spring and neap tides, mean sea level, and chart datum.

From this it will be seen that if the tidal range – from the tide tables – is ten metres it can be expected, after four hours, the tide will have fallen (or risen) by 9/12 of the range, i.e. 7.5 metres.

A further piece of information on the chart to which we shall need to refer is *variation*. Because *true north* differs from *magnetic north* by a varying amount, depending upon where you are on the earth, it is necessary to apply a correcting factor to the direction indicated by the compass. This factor, known as variation, is given on charts and maps together with the amount it varies with time. In the UK variation is about 5 degrees 20 minutes west in 1980 decreasing by about 5 minutes annually. This must be subtracted from a compass direction to obtain the true, or added to true to obtain the compass direction. The well known aide memoire:

' Variation West – Compass Best (currently applicable in UK) Variation East – Compass Least'

will help you remember whether to add or subtract. If your desired course (T) on the chart is 180 degrees and variation is, say, 5 degrees W, the course (C) is 185 degrees.

There is a further correction called *deviation* which is necessitated by the local effect of ferrous objects, notably engines in yachts, or magnetic ones such as light meters, batteries, radios etc. placed near the compass. If the canoeist takes care to keep such items well away from his compass he can forget deviation.

At this stage it may be interesting to consider an actual sea trip from Ramsgate to Margate on the Kent coast and taking in the North Foreland.

The first consideration is the state of the tides and by checking with the tide table it is found that on the day of the proposed trip the tide will be half-way between neap and spring. From the chart – Admiralty No. 1828, *The Downs* – it is found that the tidal stream will be favourable about one hour before high water at Dover, the local major port, giving a tidal stream of approximately half a knot in roughly the direction we shall be travelling. On the day in question high water at Dover is at 10.00 which means a start off the beach at Ramsgate at 09.00. The next point to check is the state of the tide at the finishing point, Margate. The distance to be covered is about eight miles and the canoeists taking part in the trip feel they can paddle this distance in two hours with the favourable tide. Thus the ETA (estimated time of arrival) at Margate will be 11.00 and referral to the chart will show a still favourable tide at this time, but during the next hour it will turn against the paddlers with a broadly adverse tidal stream of about half a knot. It will anyway be advantageous to complete the trip within three hours because three hours after high water at Dover the tidal stream will be running adversely at around one knot.

Launching will be no problem at Ramsgate since the tide will be almost high and at Margate landing will be equally easy since there is a sandy beach. What is not shown on the chart is the fact that the tidal conditions off the North Foreland can be difficult and can only be discovered by further research, or our old friend, 'local knowledge'.

Since this is a short trip, within sight of land, there is no need to have the chart available while at sea. The proposed *track* (path over the sea bed) can be plotted on the chart, the effect of the tidal stream applied to it and the *course* (direction in which you will be heading) determined. This will be a true course which must be converted to compass and noted for reference during the trip. A piece of white Formica is useful for such notes and can easily be fastened to the deck lines where it may be seen.

Against course changes, note the ETA at this point and what should be visible with its *bearing* from you. This is expressed in degrees clockwise from north. For example, we should see after approximately fifteen minutes a small bay due east, i.e. bearing 270 degrees, which is Dumpton Gap, and after another five minutes we should be abreast of Broadstairs Bay. The whole route should be plotted in this way so at any given time you are aware of what landmarks, or sea marks, should be within sight together with their bearing from you. Estimating distances is notoriously difficult at sea and more especially from a small craft like a kayak.

Bearings are normally taken *from* the observer *towards* the object observed. The exception, which is unlikely to concern canoeists, is when reporting your position to a third party, and in this case the bearing is given from the object observed towards the observer, and is normally given with an estimate of the distance. For example, my position is 90 degrees Dumpton Gap 2 miles. A bearing of, say, a clock tower, when plotted on the chart will give a *position line* somewhere along which will be your position at the time the bearing was taken. If a second bearing is taken such that the resulting position line crosses the original – the nearer a right angle the better – the point where they cross will give you a *fix* which is where you were when the fix was obtained, subject to any errors inherent in taking bearings from a small craft.

It is preferable, where possible, to obtain three bearings, the position lines of which will probably form a small triangle – the smaller the better – referred to as a 'cocked hat'. It is usual to assume your position as being the centre of the 'cocked hat' unless one corner is nearer to some point of possible danger in which case this corner should be taken as the assumed position so any error will hopefully include a safety factor. You may find it helpful to draw short lines at the beginning and end of each course line at ten

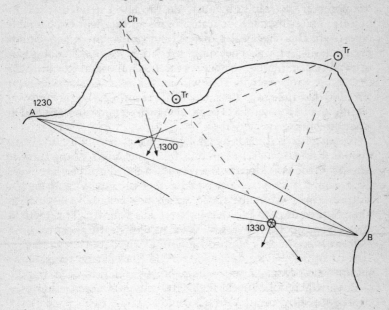

FIG. 11

A canoeist proposes to paddle across a bay from A – B and estimates the journey time to be 1½ hours. He prepares a sketch map on which the line A – B represents the course to steer; also marked are the 10 degree lines each side of the course at both ends. After 30 minutes he takes bearings of the church and the two towers, one of which is rather distant. When the three position lines are plotted he finds the tide is setting him in towards the shore more than had been anticipated and he is just about 10 degrees off course. He alters course 20 degrees to starboard which should bring him back on course after a further 30 minutes paddling. At 13.30 it is possible to obtain a transit bearing from the church and tower, plus a bearing of the second tower. These two position lines place him 10 degrees off course again but this time to the right of his course and rather ahead of time. It is a simple matter to estimate the change of course necessary to arrive at B where a slightly early arrival may now be anticipated due to the favourable tidal set.

degrees to the course (see Fig. 11). If fixes are then obtained which place you off course it is easier to estimate the correction necessary to return to the correct course.

It may be possible to obtain a single position line from a *transit* obtained when two objects on shore are in line with each other and the observer, you, are obviously on the line extended from the objects. Two simultaneous transits give an excellent fix. Suitable objects are churches, water towers, and similar prominent buildings. A transit may also be combined with a position line obtained from a bearing in order to obtain a fix. It is important to remember that the fix is related to the time when it was obtained and is relevant only for that time, i.e. a strong tidal stream may be moving you rapidly and a second fix will be needed to determine how fast and in what direction.

The *running fix* is made by taking a bearing on an object to obtain a position line and, after a suitable time has elapsed, taking another bearing on the same object. Transfer the original position line along the assumed track a distance equal to that which you estimate you will have paddled in the time elapsed between the two position lines. Where the two position lines cross is your fix. This method does depend upon more variables than straight bearing position lines or transits so the fix obtained cannot be considered very reliable.

Much of your navigation will depend on your having a reasonably accurate knowledge of your own paddling speed, so every opportunity should be taken to check this. It is possible to get a rough idea of your speed by timing yourself while paddling past a fixed object such as a mooring buoy. Start the timing as your bow is level with the object and finish as your stern passes it. Divide this time in seconds into the length of your kayak and take 2/3 of the answer to obtain your speed over the ground in miles per hour. If your kayak is 15 feet long, the equation is for feet, and you take four seconds to pass a buoy then from $2/3 \times 15/4$ your speed is 2.5 mph.

Armed with your pre-worked sheet of course notes, and perhaps a tracing off the appropriate section of the chart, you should have no problem calculating where you are at any time during the trip. In fine weather this adds interest at the least, but if the weather clamps down, as it can with disturbing suddenness, you will be well placed either to continue if this is deemed safe or be able to decide upon a suitable refuge.

The bearings of suitable refuge beaches can be noted but

remember such bearings will be based on the assumption that you are on course at the correct time – hence the need to keep a close check on this by means of transits and bearings whenever the opportunity occurs.

At the beginning of this chapter I mentioned the booklet, *The Seaway Code*. In this will be found an illustrated description of the lateral system of buoyage which is now in use around the coasts of the UK. The basic marks are those indicating the deep water channel in rivers and estuaries; port (left) hand buoys are red and can shaped, starboard (right) hand buoys are green and cone shaped. The port and starboard assumes you are entering from the sea. Cardinal marks are used to indicate a hazard and are yellow and black with varying top marks to show whether they are N, S, E, or W of the hazard. It is unlikely that the canoeist will need a detailed knowledge of these but he should be aware of their existence since they are concerned with navigation.

In the tidal rivers and estuaries where the marks are found the tides often run with considerable speed, and care must be taken to avoid hazards created by the fast moving water. For example, avoid getting too close to moored barges and ships for, as in the case with bridges on rapid rivers, it is all too easy to become jammed against or between such obstructions, with possible fatal results. The buoys, themselves, are very large indeed, and can be potential hazards in their own right to the canoeist, so in tidal waters do not underestimate the strength and speed of the tide and take care to avoid being swept into potential danger.

During the trip around the North Foreland, adverse tides were avoided by choice of time and good fortune: had the journey been longer this would probably not have been possible. At the very least the canoeists could have expected to have to contend with a tidal stream at an angle to their course. If this is the case it is necessary to allow for the distance the tide is going to sweep you off course in order to arrive at your intended destination. It will be possible to do all the work necessary to arrive at your course to steer, i.e. the compass course, before venturing on to the sea. The course being the direction in which the kayak is heading; the track being the direction it takes over the sea bed, and is the line of intended travel on the chart. Both course and track may be expressed as true (T) or compass (C). I prefer to work on the chart in true and convert only the course to compass.

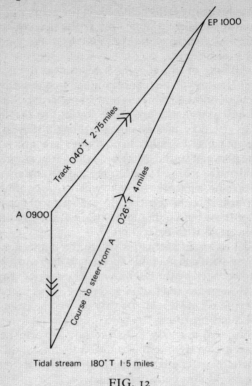

EP 1000

Track 040° T 2·75 miles

A 0900

Course to steer from A   026° T 4 miles

Tidal stream   180° T 1·5 miles

FIG. 12

Fig. 12 shows an example of how to obtain a course to steer if you know: 1) the required track; 2) the set and rate of the tide; 3) current variation, and 4) your paddling speed. Lay off on the chart from your starting point, A, the required track, in our example this is 040 degrees T, mark the track line with two arrows. Again from A lay off the set and rate of the tidal stream, 180 degrees, 1.5 miles, mark with three arrows. Assume your paddling speed is four knots and mark off the course line from the end of the tidal stream line to where a scale distance of four miles crosses the track. This gives your estimated position (EP) after one hour's paddling. The course line should be marked with one arrow and its true value when corrected for variation will give you a course to steer *from A* in order to make good the required track. The distance made good in one hour may be scaled off from A to the EP on the track line and will be found to be 2.75 miles. Obviously further plots will be required on a long trip to account for changes in the tidal stream.

Using a similar triangle of velocities it is equally possible to determine the track which will result if a certain course is steered. This is of less interest to the canoeist since it is worked afloat from necessity, normally to check that a given hazard will be cleared if the course steered is continued.

Once the required track has been taken from the chart all subsequent plotting can be done on plain paper, or better, graph paper, with distances scaled from the chart, of course. This reduces the wear and tear on the chart and the resulting courses are simply noted on the waterproof sheet as already suggested. Do not forget to convert from true on the chart to compass for use afloat.

Wind direction and speed may also affect your track but it is difficult in a kayak to make a proper allowance for this and provided you keep checking by means of fixes you should be able to make sufficient allowance during the trip.

10

Canoe Touring

Carrying your canoe by road

While petrol remains available, transporting a canoe or canoes is
relatively simple. Two or three canoes may be carried on a roof rack
– the best type being that fitted with 'V' bars into which the ends of
the canoes fit, preventing forwards or backwards movement. Then
you have only to retain the canoes in the 'V's to obtain a safe
package. The normal short roof rack is less satisfactory and, if used,
the canoe should be well braced to the front and rear bumpers of the
car to prevent it swinging sideways when buffeted by the wind at
speed.

Restrictions
There are legal limitations on the overhang allowed at both ends of
any vehicle and the current regulations, which apply to canoes, are
as follows.

1   Regarding *forward* overhang
    a) Up to 1.83 metres (6 feet) no special marking or
       arrangements.
    b) Over 1.83 metres (6 feet) and up to 3.05 metres (10 feet).
       There must be an attendant travelling in the vehicle with the
       driver.
       The overhang must be marked with a marker board.

c) With an overhang of more than 3.05 metres (10 feet) special arrangements must be made with the police, who require two clear days' notice of your movement.

2 Regarding *rearward* overhang
   a) Up to 1.07 metres (3 feet 6 in) no special marking required.
   b) Over 1.07 metres (3 feet 6 in) and up to 1.83 metres (6 feet) the overhang must be marked e.g. with a distinctive piece of cloth;
   c) Between 1.83 metres (6 feet) and 3.05 metres (10 feet) the overhang must be marked with a special marker board.
   d) Over 3.05 (10 feet) special arrangements must be made with the police.

Most canoes will come into the 'no special marking' category for with a 4 metre (13 feet) long car there is unlikely to be more than a 1 metre overhang at each end. The problem can arise with a racing canoe, but even then is likely only with the K4 which is 11 metres (36 feet 6 in) long!

Transporting more canoes than can be conveniently carried on a car roof – and do check the weight limitations for your car roof – entails the use of a trailer. Several types of canoe trailer are commercially available but it is also possible to construct your own. Whether buying or making, make sure that the structure is rigid both laterally and longitudinally when it is fully loaded. A collapsed trailer on a motorway could cause real mayhem! Check too that all bolted connections are fitted with shake-proof nuts or lock nuts; rigidity diminishes rapidly when vital nuts start to loosen.

There are restrictions on trailers towed by private cars. These are: a normal maximum length of 7 metres (23 feet), excluding the tow bar and any tow bar fittings. (This length may be extended to 12 metres (40 feet) subject to certain conditions.)

The maximum length of both vehicle and trailer must not exceed 18 metres (60 feet).

The maximum width must not exceed 2.3 metres (8 feet 6 in).

If you feel that your canoe or trailer is approaching the limitations do check the current situation with your local traffic police before setting out.

Pooling resources

The use of commercial sized vehicles for canoe transport may be considered by clubs or large groups and is particularly useful where not only the canoes but also the paddlers and their equipment can all be carried in the same vehicle. This may also ease collection problems at the end of a tour since only one driver is required. Check licence requirements, though, for the vehicle you propose using. The alternative is for two cars to be taken to the last point of the tour on the first day. Both drivers return in one car leaving the other parked to be used on the last day as a ferry for other drivers. Public transport is sometimes possible for the return on the last day but is likely to be time consuming.

The problem does not arise if there are non-canoeing drivers in the party. In this case the cars can be driven each day to meet the canoeists. This is especially helpful where you have a fixed camp from which explorations are made each day. The Spey area in Scotland offers good opportunities for this with several small but interesting rivers available, in addition to the Spey itself.

Other means of transport

With the increasing cost of fuel many canoeists now look for more economic means of transporting canoes. One which would seem to offer possibilities is carrying one or two canoes on a motor-cycle sidecar. Another, which I have used myself, is towing by bicycle. Better, perhaps, would be a cycle sidecar, since this would reduce rolling friction and avoid the problems of a long tow bar.

The repair kit

Different types of canoe equipment have already been discussed but one essential common to all is the repair kit. It is obviously impractical to carry enough equipment for major repairs while on a short trip. What you should have is the equivalent of the motorists' 'get you home' kit.

For day trips in plywood or GRP canoes some means of sealing cracks is most important since cracks are the most commonly encountered repairable damage. The stressed skin type of plywood construction, such as the DK, has resilience similar to that of GRP construction but is obviously rather less tough unless clad with resin and glass cloth or mat.

If the plywood shell of this type is split the edges of the crack will normally open on the outside so, where possible, the split should be held together with copper wire or nylon fishing line 'stitches'. The repair kit should therefore include some suitable copper wire or nylon fishing line of about 18 kg (40 lb) breaking strain, and a curved upholsterer's needle to thread the line, even where it is not possible to reach the interior. Also required is a small brad awl for making the 'stitch' holes.

With the edges of the split held together some means of sealing is required. The best is the tape which was developed for pipe sealing on North Sea oil rigs – this is only obtainable from McNulty Seaglass Ltd., (see address list), at present, though no doubt other canoe stockists and makers will be supplying it soon. This tape will seal cracks in GRP hulls, although if the cracks are extensive they may require further reinforcement.

You can make GRP repairs on the river bank but this is not worthwhile if a satisfactory temporary repair can be made more quickly. (Permanent repairs will be considered in the next chapter on maintenance.)

Camping equipment

Touring in a canoe almost always means camping for it is unlikely that you will be able to find overnight accommodation at suitable intervals on the most desirable canoeing rivers. Essentials are some form of overnight shelter, a sleeping bag, and a means of cooking.

Shelter
The shelter can be as simple as a plastic sheet or as complicated as the latest thing in lightweight tents. A reasonable compromise is one of the many light nylon or cotton tents currently available. This will not be cheap but with care it will last several years and ensure dry nights which are always welcome after a wet day on the river. Nylon dries quickly and is lighter than cotton but has the disadvantage of allowing some condensation inside and probably has a shorter waterproof life than cotton.

When choosing a sleeping bag there are currently three options open to you – natural down, the best and most expensive but it *must* be kept dry; one of the synthetic fillings such as *Hollofil* which are heavier and less compressible than down, but cheaper and retain their insulating properties better when wet; and, thirdly, a bag made from one of the synthetic pile materials. This is reputed to retain its warmth even when wet and could be worthy of consideration although it may be bulkier when packed. What you buy will depend upon personal taste. One of the synthetic alternatives is probably a better buy than a cheap feather and down-filled bag.

Cooking

Camp cooking can be quick and simple with the introduction of 'meals' which require only the addition of hot water for their reconstitution and cooking.

Some form of stove is essential for trying to light a cooking fire in cold, wet conditions is miserable and there is currently a good choice of lightweight stoves on the market. The choice depends, in the main, on the type of fuel used although there is now one – the American MSR multi-fuel stove – which will burn petrol, paraffin, diesel fuel, white spirit and aviation fuel. However, it is more expensive than standard stoves.

Cheaper, and more common, are the small butane or propane gas stoves which are convenient although their small gas cartridges are relatively expensive. The traditional paraffin pressure stoves are excellent, but fairly expensive, and rather slower to get going; they are good for fast cooking. The petrol stove has similar advantages, but some campers are not entirely happy with petrol as a cooking fuel. Finally, there are spirit stoves burning either solid or liquid methylated spirit. These are inexpensive to buy but are rather slow and expensive to run if you propose doing a lot of cooking.

The best of these, I think, is the *Trangia,* or the *Optimus,* which incorporates a windshield/pot holder which concentrates the heat on to the bottom and sides of the pots. The *Trangia* can be bought in two sizes with one or two cooking pans, an optional kettle, and a frying pan which forms the lid. The whole lot straps together to form a convenient cooking outfit. For the simple cooking usually adopted on tour I favour the *Trangia,* but do check what is available and decide what will best suit your requirements.

Other items will be obvious – do remember to take a tin opener, the 'Baby' type can be kept on a key ring.

When buying or making gear bear in mind that weight is less

important for the canoeist than bulk for, unless you have one of the larger 'touring' kayaks or an open canoe, you will find space under the decks of the modern kayak fairly limited.

Clothes

Clothing for paddling is very much a personal choice with some form of light footwear essential to cope with whatever type of bank or shore you may have to land on. Light basket-ball type canvas boots are good for rocky conditions where it is often necessary to wade through shallows for they offer some protection to ankles. Wellingtons or the similar boots worn by dinghy sailors are unsuitable for the kayak cockpit where they may jam and prevent your easy exit.

Loading your equipment

When you have gathered together all the gear required for your tour you will need to decide how to pack it into the canoe. Top priority is keeping the equipment dry. Waterproof bags are the answer. These may be specially bought, but heavy gauge plastic bags are satisfactory if they are treated with care to avoid splits. Single bags can be made reasonably watertight by folding and tying the neck tightly and dryness for the gear is assured if two bags are used, one inside the other. Do not overfill the bags or squeeze all the air from them as trapped air will add buoyancy.

Generally it is better to pack items in several small bags rather than a few large ones. Smaller bags are easier to fit into the canoe and, in the event of one bag leaking, fewer items get wet. Also available from canoeing suppliers are cylindrical plastic containers with screw caps. These are especially useful for emergency requirements. some repair outfits are sold in such containers. Pack into the canoe first those items which will be needed last on your arrival at your camp site – for example, you are unlikely to need your sleeping bag until after the tent is erected, but spare clothes may be required during the day either to change into after a capsize or to go shopping. A lunch box and flask containing a hot drink or soup can usually be fitted in at the side of the seat in a kayak but avoid having anything packed into the cockpit area where it could hinder your escape in an emergency.

If you have inflated buoyancy bags you may have difficulty in fitting both these and your camping equipment into the kayak, especially in the bow where space is more restricted. Your sleeping bag in two watertight bags will form an adequate bow bouyancy bag and should fit in front of the footrest to which it should be secured. Spare clothes may also fit into the bow, or behind the seat and in front of the tent and cooking equipment. Unless you have a very bulky tent you will probably find the stern bouyancy bag can be held in position, and a loosely packed tent in waterproof bags will provide some bouyancy in itself.

Packing the canoe satisfactorily is not difficult and experience will show you which items fit best in which positions. Arrange the weight so the canoe floats with normal trim, i.e. with the bow and stern in the correct relative positions even if a little lower in the water than usual. Ideally the canoe should be packed afloat since carrying a loaded canoe may be difficult and, if heavily loaded, might break the back of the canoe.

Choosing the camp site

If camping arrangements have not already been made it is important to ensure that a suitable site is found near the river. It may be best to stop at a good site even though you have arrived there in the early afternoon when you would normally feel it too early to stop for the day. It is better to make camp in good time rather than be frantically seeking a site at dusk.

Islands may at first seem a good choice but in fact they usually harbour a large variety of winged, biting insects which will put in an unwelcome appearance after you have set up camp. Biting insects are a hazard of any waterside camp but islands excel in the variety they provide! Already mentioned is the danger of the mountain-fed river which may rise very rapidly to overflow its banks – and your camp site – in just a few hours. Try to find a pitch for your tent which is likely to be above such floods.

Coastal cruising has its own problems of which the most pressing is that of finding a suitable pitch for the tent with reasonable access to the sea. Each section of coast presents its own difficulties although the East coast is easier in some ways than the more rugged West. Forward planning is essential in this as in all aspects of sea canoeing for you do not want to finish the day at the foot of a sea cliff with a rising tide and no place to land, quite apart from setting up camp.

Trial runs

Having tried packing your canoe with all the gear you feel is necessary to enjoy a comfortable canoe touring holiday, a trial weekend on some local water is an excellent idea. Make this first trial run as simple as possible by going out and finding a suitable camp site before you start. Check that launching is possible at the start and there is a place for landing and loading the car at the end. This introduction to canoe touring is made easier if you become a member of the Canoe Camping Club or a local canoe touring club, for you can then take part in one of their organised meets and will not need to do much of the preparatory work.

Holiday tours

During your first tour you will find which items of equipment are essential and which can be left at home. There is little point in carrying something around the countryside just in case it may some day be needed. The exceptions are the first aid box, the repair kit for the canoe, and safety equipment for use in tidal waters.

Where you go for your holiday depends entirely upon your personal requirements. The Spey has already been mentioned. More staid, but equally interesting in its own way, is the Severn, or you may prefer the beauty of one of the west country rivers whose tidal waters offer excellent opportunities for canoeing holidays, provided the usual precautions applicable to sea canoeing are taken on the broader estuaries. Few of the west country rivers are worth trying to canoe above their tidal limits, as they are often shallow and rock strewn in summer, and are much used by fishermen.

East coast canoeists have a greater choice of rivers, but many of these, especially in the south, are gentle and once the estuary is reached low tide may reveal acres of mud to be negotiated before a landing can be achieved. A tide table is essential.

Ireland offers good possibilities since access is less of a problem than in the UK and there is some good and varied canoeing water.

Those wishing to venture abroad will find much of canoeing interest in France where tributaries of the Rhône, such as the Ardèche, offer good canoeing and the promise of fine weather too. The Rhône itself has been made less interesting by the building of barrages which must be portaged.

Several travel companies offer canoe holidays abroad and could be a good introduction both to the sport and foreign canoeing. Details will be found in a current copy of *Canoeing Magazine*.

11

Repair and Maintenance

The repair and maintenance of canoes is normally a reasonably straightforward job. If the repair work is more akin to a complete rebuild – and it is possible to rebuild a canoe which has broken in half – then whether it is worthwhile may be questionable.

GRP repairs

For all work involving the cutting, grinding or glass-papering of GRP, a face mask should be worn to avoid the breathing or ingestion of GRP dust.

Typical damage occurring to GRP canoes are holes made on impact with rocks and other canoes etc; splits in the hull-deck seam; end damage, usually from impact; and damage to the seat-cockpit area, possible from bad usage. First make sure that the area of damage is clean and dry. Remove salt with fresh water. If a patch is to be applied to the smooth, external gel coat, this should first be 'keyed' by rubbing down with a coarse glass paper.

Repairing holes

Holes can be mended in a number of ways according to the type and extent of the damage. Often the hole can be reached from the inside through the cockpit sometimes with difficulty and a brush on the end of a stick. This is always preferable to working from the outside only. If the hole is small, tidy it by pressing out any impacted laminate and removing any loose pieces. Tape over the outside of the hole a piece of card covered with *Melinex* or *Sellotape* for small repairs to prevent sticking. (The coating should be face down, i.e. in contact with the canoe skin.) Wet out the area of the hole from the inside of the canoe, if possible, using gel coat. Then build up a patch starting with a piece of chopped strand glass mat about the same size as the hole. Successive layers of mat should each be larger until the patch is a little thicker than the skin and extends outside the area of damage by about 25 mm (1 in) or so. The mat should be wetted out with normal lay-up resin to ensure a non-sticky finish inside.

If the hole is too large for the card to lie flat over it, you will first have to make a mould from a similar shaped section of the hull – possibly from the other side of the canoe or perhaps from another canoe of the same design. To make the mould, clean and polish the area from which it is to be taken and coat with a release agent. Apply a gel coat then leave until it becomes tacky. Build up on this two or three layers of chopped strand glass mat, wetting out with lay-up resin. Allow this to 'cure' before removing.

Coat the inside of the mould with release agent and tape it into position over the hole as described above. The repair is then dealt with in the same way.

Repairing splits

Splits at the gunwales require an internal patch extending well across the underside of the deck and hull where the split has occurred. It may be necessary to hold the edges of the split together, and this can be achieved by tying a rope round the hull at this point, but not so tight that the shape is distorted. Having completed the repair on the inside it may be worthwhile taping along both gunwales on the outside if you don't mind the appearance of the tape.

Repairing the end

The type of damage at the ends of canoes depends on whether they are over-rich in resin or not. If the mat has been well wetted into the ends, as it should be, damage will be confined to cracking or splintering. This can easily be built up again by working a little lay-up resin into the damage area. When this has cured, the end can be finished to the correct profile with resin paste, pigmented to match the hull/deck colour.

If the end is resin-rich hard knocks will tend to break off pieces of cured resin which may expose the mat beneath. (If the mat is *not* exposed the end can be built up as described above.) If the mat is exposed it may be better to refashion the end so that it is blunter and, consequently, less susceptible to damage rather than try to rebuild it to its original profile. In any event exposed mat should be protected as soon as possible to prevent water seeping into the lamination.

Repairing the seat-cockpit

In the seat-cockpit area most damage probably comes from ill usage, such as standing on the seat when getting into the canoe. Splits in the seat itself are easily repaired by applying patches to the underside of the damaged area. It may also be worthwhile adding a plywood strut under the seat glass taped to the hull and the seat.

Cockpit damage may be in the form of cracks across the coaming caused by an unnatural load e.g. encountered in surfing, or perhaps the coaming parting company from the deck. Coaming repairs will probably have to be made on the outside if a spray cover is used after the repair work. Glass tape is useful for this type of repair and can also be used if the coaming is coming away from the deck. Clean the crack and work in some resin – epoxy is best – to the broken joint before taping over the damaged area. Again it will be necessary to work from inside the cockpit to avoid spoiling the coaming for the spray cover.

Repairs to plywood

Plywood canoes are less robust than those made from GRP and their repair may be more difficult. It is virtually impossible to rebuild a plywood canoe which has broken into two. However, if appearance is not too important, quite sound repairs can be made with glass mat and resin.

Repairs to holes

The basic impact hole is likely to affect the plywood canoe less than the GRP type simply because when plywood is hit by a sharp object it is more likely to split than form a hole. The split will leak, of course, and still requires repair. If several square centimetres are damaged it is best to cut out the damaged area by removing a regularly shaped piece of ply, e.g. a square. A new piece of plywood of the same thickness is then cut to the exact shape of the piece which has been removed, using the damaged piece as a template, and fitted into the hole.

Cut a second piece of plywood 2 or 3 cm (1 in) larger all round than the replacement piece, and fit inside the hull to hold the patch in place. Scrape away any paint or varnish round the hole on the inside of the hull before the larger piece of plywood is glued into position. To ensure a really tight fit this piece should be pinned into position with brass panel pins; if the area is one with a marked curvature 'Gripfast' nails should be used. (Ignore the points on the outside at this stage.) If even the 'Gripfast' nails do not hold the plywood closely enough wedge it into position with short pieces of scrap wood but do ensure that the opposite side is protected from the resulting pressure by placing another piece of scrap wood under the end of the wedge.

Clean around the edges of the hole on the outside while the glue is still soft – or the patching piece will not fit – then leave the plywood in position until the glue has hardened. Once the glue has set, the patch can be glued into position and again it may be necessary to nail or wedge it into the correct shape. Wooden wedges forced under a rope around the hull will probably be sufficient if you do not wish to use nails. Finally cut off the points of the nails, if they have been used, and fill any small cracks with waterproof filler before painting or varnishing. If done carefully this repair will be undetectable from the outside and the canoe will be as strong as it was before the accident.

Smaller damage can be repaired quite adequately by applying a mixture of resin and chopped strand mat cut into small pieces. The mixture is worked well into the damaged area without attempting to get a good finish. When the resin is cured it can be glass papered down flush with the surrounding skin and finished to match. The interior can be left rough or finished according to choice and ease of access.

Repairing splits

Split gunwales are unusual but may occur when trying to empty a kayak full of water when it is possible for the deck to pull away at the gunwale joint. In this case the best remedy is to rebuild the section of gunwale affected if the deck itself is undamaged.

Carefully lift the deck away from the damaged area by easing a knife blade or chisel under it. Wash away any salt or dirt and allow to dry. Time can be saved here by using a hair dryer. Next, clean the joint of any loose glue, remove pins and nails from the affected area, and re-glue using pins or nails in different places to ensure good holding. The result should be nearly as good as new. It may be possible to glass tape the outside of the gunwales, as is done on the DK plywood designs, or even to apply a layer of glass mat on the inside of the gunwale, between the deck and hull. Care will be needed though to ensure a good joint if the gunwale strip has a sharp edge for this will make it difficult to get the mat into the corners thus formed.

Repairing the cockpit

It is unlikely that cockpit damage will occur in a plywood canoe unless it is combined with much more extensive damage when the whole question of the economy of the repair will have to be considered.

If a plywood hull is quite sound the deck can be replaced. With the DK designs it should be possible to re-use the original cockpit coaming with new deck sections providing the coaming is un-damaged. The cockpit area is very strong on these designs because the coaming is made of moulded plywood which is an integral part of the deck and which is, in turn, fastened to the two deck support frames. Deck damage is therefore likely to be confined to the areas fore and aft of the cockpit where strength is provided only by the thickness of the plywood and its curvature. For sea use, resin-glass mat laminate can be applied to the underside of the foredeck to strengthen this to facilitate deep water rescues.

Scrapes and scratches

Scrapes and scratches on both GRP and plywood canoes are inevitable and can be filled with a resin paste, such as *Plastic Padding,* as necessary. Care should be taken to keep the paint or varnish skin of plywood craft intact to prevent the entry of water for this can seep beneath the paint unseen (but on varnished hulls leaves a dark stain) and eventually the coating will lift and rot set in.

Epoxy resins, such as *Araldite,* are useful for repairing very small holes or scratches because their adhesive properties are better than those of polyester resins used for gel coats and lay-up.

Repairing equipment

Frequent inspection of all your canoeing gear should be a regular activity, and most repairs are a matter of common sense.

Paddles

Paddles can be repaired depending on the scale of the damage. A plastics or wooden blade in a tubular loom can be replaced, or both blades can be fitted to a new loom if the original is bent or run over, or otherwise written off. If a wooden blade breaks from a laminated wooden loom there is not very much that can be done to save it. Theoretically it is possible to scarf the blade back on to the loom but whether such a repair would stand the strain of paddling is dubious.

If the loom breaks in the centre – convenient but unlikely – the paddle could be shortened and a new scarf joint made, or perhaps more practical, the ends of the break could be sawn off clean and a pair of ferrules fitted so the paddle could be carried as a spare when touring.

Split blades used to be fairly common when blades were carved from solid spruce but are now rarely seen with the advent of laminated or plywood blades. Some of the plastics type deteriorate with age and then tend to break relatively easily – they are, of course, not repairable.

Chipped blades can be repaired and strengthened by glass taping. This may be useful on new blades if you frequent shallow, rocky streams.

12

An Introduction to Canoe Sport

When canoeing was in its infancy skills were minimal and it was possible to use the same canoe for touring, rough water, sea canoeing, or even sprint racing. As skills developed in the various aspects of the sport the demand for more responsive and specialised canoes increased, and was reflected in the manufacturers' designs. In some areas of the sport new, and sometimes quite radically changed, designs are appearing each year. This is not to say that every change is for the better, either for canoeing in general, or for one facet of the sport in particular. Ultimately, the customer must decide which craft is best for him.

It is significant that more manufacturers are now producing craft specifically designed for touring, the sporting canoe having grown so specialised that it is now unsuitable for touring purposes.

The BCU is of course responsible for the sporting side of canoeing in Britain and has a Sports Management Committee which oversees the competitive sphere of the sport; there are also specialist committees dealing with each aspect of canoeing, and provision has recently been made for the appointment of nine honorary Regional Racing Coaches to advise locally on all aspects of competitive canoeing.

To make a start in canoe sport it is almost essential to belong to a club for it is at club level where you can begin to enjoy competition. Not all aspects of canoe sport are mutually exclusive – slalom competition has much in common with wild water racing and is more akin to surf canoeing than ordinary sea canoeing.

Slalom competitions are usually organised on a section of wild water, sometimes below a weir on an otherwise staid river, such as the Thames, but more often on a wild water river. The course is laid out with pairs of poles forming 'gates' hanging from overhead wires, and the slalomist has to negotiate the course through and around the 'gates', forwards and backwards, in the shortest possible time, without touching the poles. Capsizes are not penalised other than by the increased time taken, but hitting a pole, passing a 'gate' in the wrong direction, or omitting one completely are all subject to penalties.

A very specialised type of kayak has evolved for slalom with low, flat ends which can be ducked under poles where there may be a danger of hitting one (see Figure 4, p. 11). The keel line is well rockered but the bottom is fairly flat in cross section so when the canoeist wishes to turn really fast he will lay the canoe on to its side to take advantage of the greater curve of the gunwale on which to turn. Rear decks are very flat so that the Steyr roll, which requires the paddler to lean right back on the rear deck, can be used. The foredeck may be flattish or relatively high depending on the type of water the kayak has been designed for. Very rough water – 'white water' – gains its appearance from a multitude of air bubbles, which do not support the canoe as well as more 'solid' water, hence the need for a more buoyant kayak for use in white water.

Bow and stern on the more extreme designs are very flat and offer no buoyancy, being, in reality, mere appendages to enable the craft to conform to the minimum length rule – currently 4 metres. This kind of non-essential development in canoe design could probably be eliminated in slalom kayaks by introducing a rule which did not permit hollow lines – the ends would then have to have at least a slightly convex keel line.

In addition to the single seat K 1 slalom kayaks discussed, there are also C 1 and C 2 slalom canoes. These are fully decked craft with near round cockpits in which the paddler kneels in order to wield his single bladed paddle to best advantage. Although of greater beam than the K 1 slalom kayak, the shape of the C 1, and to a lesser extent the C 2, is evolving closer to that of the K 1, and they certainly bear little similarity to the open touring canoes. Handling a C 1 in rough water is more difficult than the K 1, but the skilled canoeist gains great satisfaction from the mastery of his craft.

The C 2 is, perhaps, the most versatile of the wild water craft in the hands of two really proficient paddlers. Like the other slalom craft, it can be rolled but this obviously requires full co-operation between the crew!

Slalom canoe sport is probably best known to the general public from television. If it appeals to you, do not rush off to buy the most extreme example of slalom craft you can find in the hope of becoming a first-class paddler. Visit some slaloms and talk to the competitors, especially those just out of the novice class for they will be able to tell you of the most suitable designs currently available for the newcomer.

You should by now be a member of a club and so will not find it too difficult to see, and try, some of the craft which appeal to you. Having found your ideal craft – at least for this year – do make sure you can be comfortable in it. Is the seat the right shape for you? Can the footrest to adjusted to your size? Is it buoyant enough for your weight?

As a beginner you will start by entering the novice events before being promoted to Division 3 in the ranking lists. Success in Division 3 brings promotion to Division 2, and, finally, to Division 1. Ladies have their own divisions and promotion system. Progress through the ranking lists demands considerable dedication to the sport involving, as it does, considerable travel to attend the various slalom courses. However, this will not deter the real slalom enthusiast!

Surf competition

Good surf beaches are less common than slalom river courses in Britain and so surf competition is less common. As we have already discovered it is possible to surf in almost any kayak but there is a specialist craft for the expert. This is the surf shoe, which is a little like a cross between a kayak and a surf board. It is of little use for any other purpose than surfing but it does excel at this.

Wild water racing

Wild water racing is usually a straight race against the clock down a particularly interesting white water section of a river. This can be made even more interesting by the opening of sluices, where these are available. A few years ago slalom craft were used for this type of race, but these lack the waterline length to achieve good forward speeds and now specialist craft have been developed which have more in common with sprint racing than slalom.

It is not normally necessary to be a ranking slalomist before being accepted as an entrant in most of the better known races.

Generally, wild water races are held in the winter, and wet suits are usually mandatory. For all wild water canoeing on river or at sea a protective helmet should be worn.

Marathon racing

Marathon racing (formerly called long distance racing, and re-named by the International Canoe Federation (ICF)) is a term which can apply to races which are held on rivers – including tidal estuaries – canals, or a combination of any or all of these. The best known marathon race in England is the Devizes to Westminster Race held at Easter each year. This is a canal, river and tideway course, 125 miles long.

The officially agreed classes for marathon racing are the same as those use for flat water racing – K 1, K 2, C 1 and C 2, although some thought is being given to the design of the C classes since the existing flat water designs are unsuited to most marathon courses. Most marathon race organisers also include classes for wild water craft and specific fast touring craft of the type known as Class 3 (single seat) and Class 4 (two seat) in Britain. It will be seen that marathon racing should offer the opportunity for those canoeists without an extreme specialist craft to try competitive canoeing.

Flat water or sprint racing

The sprint canoeist is concerned only with getting to the finish line in less time than his competitors. This is not say that canoeing technique is any less important but the water is always flat, subject to wind conditions, and the craft, although they may be used for marathon racing and even lightweight touring, are better suited to calm water.

The top class sprint craft are made from moulded wood veneers which produces a beautiful but expensive boat. There are five classes, K 1, K 2, K 4, C 1, and C 2, raced over distances of 500 metres, 1,000 metres and 10,000 metres with junior, ladies, and senior races.

To conform to the minimum beam rules, most racing craft have a diamond plan shape with the maximum beam at only one point well behind the cockpit which gives a minimum waterline beam commensurate with stability and the volume necessary to support the paddler.

This then is the competitive side of canoeing. Many canoeists compete in more than one form – surfing in the summer and slalom during the winter, for example – while the marathon racer may well be a flat water enthusiast too. If you aspire to the upper echelons of the sport, though, undivided devotion will be required for standards are rising and the competition to get to the top becomes tougher each year.

Join a club and have a go – you may just find yourself in the next Olympics!

13

Instruction and Coaching

In this chapter are brief details of the formal structure of canoe instruction and testing currently available in the UK. There may be organisations I have inadvertently omitted – my apologies to them if this has occurred.

Many enthusiasts began canoeing by having their interest aroused from a book. They then moved to the purchase or making of a canoe. Before 1950 there was little choice. In the 1930s, the Scout movement published designs for two canvas-covered kayaks and had some involvement in the training of young canoeists, but it was not until the British Canoe Union Coaching Scheme was inaugurated that a formal system of training and testing became available. The present proficiency tests are based on the first proficiency test which was introduced in about 1949. The National Coaching Committee was established in 1961. From this has developed the present Coaching Scheme, which is administered by the National Coaching and Development Committee, headed by the Director of Coaching and Development, and overseen by the Access, Coaching and Recreation Management Committee.

Coaching panels have been set up with Regional Coaching Organisers (RCO) managing each region of the country. They are assisted by Local Coaching Organisers (LCO) in sub-divisions of the regions. Individual canoeists are put into contact with the LCO or RCO who will then be able to offer advice on the local and national aspects of canoe training and testing. Most people in the Scheme are, of course, voluntary workers.

The Scheme is now used, in one way or another, by most of the organisations which include canoeing among their activities. The range of coaching extends from the basic elementary test – One Star – for the beginner, to the advanced tests on river or sea. In addition there are, for those members of the BCU wishing to join the Coaching Scheme, coaching awards which are designed to prepare proficient canoeists for the training and testing of others.

The initial award is the probationary one of Trainee Instructor which is made on the successful completion of a short training course. The Trainee then has to pass an assessment weekend after a minimum of six months as a trainee, during which period he will have been expected to have assisted with canoe training. Details of training ind assessment courses are avialable from LCOs, RCOs and the BCU.

Currently there are two types of tests of canoeing competence. The Star Tests are intended to test individual skills from the One Star elementary level to the Five Star advanced level – the latter being divided (as is the Four Star) into wild-water or surfing techniques. While the Proficiency Tests are intended after the Elementary Test which is the same as the One Star, to test the ability of the candidate as a touring canoeist. There is an expedition requirement for each of the Proficiency Tests. Passing the appropriate Proficiency Test is a mandatory requirement for those wishing to enter the Coaching Scheme.

It is not necessary to become a member of the BCU to take the Tests and there is no fee for the Star Tests. Fees for the Proficiency Tests are reduced for members. Successful candidates for the Star Tests may purchase badges and certificates; cloth Proficiency badges are also available. In all cases it may be necessary to pay the examiner's expenses.

The current Proficiency Tests are:

Elementary – kayak or canoe;
Inland Proficiency Test – kayak or canoe;
Sea Proficiency Test – kayak only;
Inland Advanced Test – kayak or canoe;
Sea Advanced Test – kayak only.

Full information is obtainable from the BCU; when writing for

information to the BCU or any of the organisations whose addresses
are given on p. 120 do enclose a stamped, addressed envelope for
your reply.

The Corps of Canoe Life Guards

The Corps of Canoe Life Guards was formed after the East Coast
floods of 1953 when it was thought that trained canoeists could have
been very useful in such an emergency. More generally now they
assist life guards on the beaches round our coasts during the
summer.

At present there are three grades of membership for the Corps:
Bronze Standard for those aged fifteen years and over; Silver
Standard for those aged over seventeen; and Gold Standard for
those aged over nineteen years. The Standards are closely allied to
the BCU Proficiency and Coaching Awards and are in some ways an
extension of these especially for young people wishing to become
involved in a form of community service. Further details are
available from the BCU.

British Schools Canoeing Association

Following a meeting at the National Canoeing Exhibition at Crystal
Palace, February 1970, the British Schools Canoeing Association
was formed with the intention of developing the competitive
aspects of canoeing for young people. One of the first items on the
BSCA agenda was the organising of events for the new Espada K 1,
a 1961 design by Jorgen Samson adopted by the BCU as a 'one-
design' racing kayak in which youngsters could start their sprint or
marathon racing careers. There are Espada awards at three levels.

The BSCA has expanded its activities to all aspects of the sport
and has been closely associated with the BCU in the development of
the Star Tests.

By 1972 the BSCA Cadet one-design kayak was available to act as
a basic training craft suitable for rolling instruction as well as sea
and inland touring. In 1977 the BSCA introduced its series of
Expedition Awards to encourage its members to undertake 'pur-
poseful journeys by canoe after appropriate training has taken place
and full preparations made'.

There are three sections to each of the three levels of the Awards:

1 Attainment of the necessary skills as shown by the passing of the BCU tests;
2 Preparation, including having a purpose for the journey, and training;
3 The expedition itself and the recording of its details.

The three levels of the Award are:

1 Adventure Award (Bronze);
2 Explorer Award (Silver);
3 Voyageur Award (Gold).

Further details may be obtained from the BSCA Expedition Awards Secretary whose address can be obtained from the BCU on receipt of the usual SAE.

Duke of Edinburgh Award Scheme

The Duke of Edinburgh Award Scheme offers opportunities for young people to engage in canoeing in three of the four possible sections.

1 In the Service section a Canoe Safety Test is proposed for Bronze level while at Silver and Gold the Corps of Canoe Life Guards offer acceptable standards for candidates aspiring to these levels.
2 In the Physical Recreation section points are gained by participation; personal improvement, and performance. Bronze level requires the acquisition of 24 points; Silver – 30 points, and the Gold level – 36 points. Points may be gained for performance in the BCU Star and Proficiency Tests, and for participation in various competitive aspects of canoeing.
3 In the Expedition section of the Award all entrants have to undergo preliminary training before becoming eligible to begin work at the chosen level.

At Bronze level the candidate must have passed the BCU Proficiency Test, or the Three Star Test, and demonstrate a knowledge of expedition canoeing to the satisfaction of the assessor; or show an equivalent standard.

At the Silver and Gold levels candidates must have passed the BCU Proficiency Test and satisfy the assessor as to their competence; or show an equivalent standard.

For further details of the Scheme as applicable to canoeing the Award Handbook and the new syllabus should be consulted.

The Scout and Girl Guides Associations

The Scout Association offers its members canoeing badges at proficiency and instructor level. While these are similar in content to the BCU tests and awards they are different and any reader requiring details of them should refer to the Scout Association.

The Girl Guides does not currently have a specific canoeing badge but canoeing is included in the Boatswain Badge at a standard roughly equivalent to the One Star.

The Boys' Brigade

The Boys' Brigade formed a canoeing club in 1970 to develop all aspects of canoeing within the Brigade. The BB awards a canoeing badge which is achieved in three stages. For the first stage the candidate has to be aged at least thirteen and the test corresponds to the BCU One Star Test.

The second stage requires a minimum age of fourteen and a more advanced test is taken involving a one day expedition – this does not have an exact BCU equivalent. The third stage involves a two day expedition and is broadly the equivalent of the BCU Proficiency Test.

Other training schemes

There is a further source of formal training open, principally to adults, and this is the local evening class programme. As I write such programmes are being 'squeezed' by the present economic situation but many authorities have offered canoeing in the past and may well do so again in the future.

In addition there are a number of centres which include canoeing among the activities offered. These usually work towards the BCU standards and, where required, can often offer to test for the BCU Tests or Awards.

14

Making a Canoe

At present there are two methods of canoe construction in common use – glass fibre reinforced plastics, and plywood. Both are suitable for amateur construction. Other methods have been discussed but apart from moulded veneer craft, used primarily for racing, GRP reigns supreme with plywood construction holding its own particularly among home builders requiring one canoe for their own use.

Other than the materials used, the chief difference between these two methods is that for a GRP craft a female mould is normally required before work can begin on the actual canoe while with plywood no mould is necessary.

There are exceptions in both cases. It is possible to build a GRP canoe on a fairly simple male mould by building up the resin-glass laminate over a layer of rigid foam plastics 'planks' curved over the mould. This is fairly common for building 'one-off' yachts but is unlikely to be worthwhile for canoe construction.

It is also possible to mould a plywood craft over a similar male mould by using narrow strips of either thin wood veneers or plywood – three layers are usual for small craft, the first at an angle to the keel line, the second at right angles to this, and the third either at right angles again or parallel to the keel line. The layers may be glued with an ordinary water-resistant resin-based glue, such as *Cascamite*, or, more expensively, by using an epoxy resin. The latter method can produce a virtually rot-proof craft with strength characteristics which are probably better than a similar GRP construction.

The wood-epoxy method (not necessarily only moulded construction) has been well developed by the Gougeon Brothers in America and is called the WEST System (Wood Epoxy Saturation Technique) and uses specially developed epoxy resins of varying consistencies depending upon their required use. In the WEST System every surface of the timber used is coated with resin to exclude all moisture and while the moulded technique is not the only construction method for which it can be used it does produce an excellent craft. Details of the WEST System and the epoxy resins are available in Britain – see address list p. 122. At least one canoe design is available for moulded veneer construction by the amateur should the method appeal to you.

Building a GRP canoe

The mould
The first requirement for building the GRP canoe is the acquisition of a suitable mould. This should be borrowed or hired as making one is both prohibitively expensive and time consuming. Some resin suppliers hire moulds and enquiries should be made as to what designs are available. Your local canoe club may also have a mould or two for the use of members. Before you begin do try the canoe which is produced on the mould you are offered to ensure that it suits you.

Building your own GRP canoe is only inexpensive in relation to the cost of the commercially bought craft, it is still quite an expensive business and costs will increase as resin prices rise with upward spiralling oil prices. It is fairly common for clubs to have a number of building sessions during the winter. This brings the advantage of both bulk buying the materials and having on hand an experienced builder.

Where to build
If you can build with the local club the problem of building space is solved. You will require a space rather longer than the finished length of your proposed canoe and wide enough to allow easy access to both sides. For all but the longer racing canoes most garages are

big enough, though not ideal. Heating will be necessary in the winter to raise the internal temperature to 15–25°C (60–80°F) to ensure that the resin cures satisfactorily. (The higher the temperature the quicker the resin mixture will cure. It is obviously necessary to match the mixture and temperature to your speed of working to ensure a good result.)

Resins

You will need two types of polyester resin – a gel coat, which will provide the hard, impervious exterior of the canoe, and marine grade lay-up resin used to wet out the glasscloth or mat. Both are normally clear but can be obtained pre-coloured or you can add pigment at the mixing stage. They may also be bought pre-accelerated. You will not then need to add an accelerator. However, such resins have a more limited shelf life. Resin suppliers will give details applicable to their own products.

The catalyst

To start the curing process a catalyst (or hardener) is needed. This is available in paste or liquid form; both are equally satisfactory if used with care. But *the hardener must never be mixed directly with the accelerator since the mixture may result in an explosion.* This, in itself, is a good reason for buying pre-accelerated resin. Protect exposed skin and use barrier creams or protective gloves. Further information on the use of all GRP materials is available from the resin suppliers.

Other equipment

It is usual to colour the resin and a large range of pigments is available varying in price according to the colour. In addition to the materials for the canoe itself, you will also require release agents, liquid and wax for coating the interior of the mould to ensure that your canoe will come out and to protect the mould. Solvent will be needed for cleaning brushes and wetting out rollers, and of course the barrier cream or gloves for each member of the building team. Plastic gloves offer good protection and are cheap enough to throw away if they get torn.

The glass fibre used for boat construction is available in a variety of forms. Most common is chopped strand mat, which consists of short lengths of glass fibre held in mat form by a resin-compatible binder. Mat accepts resin well and is measured by weight, usual weights being 1 oz, 1½ oz and 2 oz per square foot. Three layers of 1 oz or two of 1½ oz are normal weight lay-up for canoe construction.

Woven roving is a heavy form of coarsely woven cloth not commonly used in canoe construction. It is measured in ounces per square yard, thus 8 oz woven roving is a little lighter than 1 oz mat. Other types of glass fibre cloth are available – curtain material, for example, and tape – but these again are not usually used for GRP canoe construction.

Tools

Certain tools will be needed.

Brushes should be considered expendable and bought at the rate of one or two for each canoe being built. 50 mm (2 in) and 100 mm (4 in) are useful sizes.

Rollers are required for wetting out the resin-mat laminate to ensure the resin is worked well into the mat without air bubbles.

An old *chisel* is useful for cleaning cured splashes of resin from the mould flanges where hull and deck are bolted together before being joined.

Trimming knives with spare blades are needed for cutting the laminate back to the flange edges. This is done when the lay-up is 'green', i.e. before it is completely cured, and so avoids the need for working on the cured laminate which creates dust and necessitates the use of a face mask.

A selection of *files* and *rasps* will be found useful as will a *powered sander* – but do wear an appropriate face mask when using these.

Construction

The construction procedure is quite straightforward and full details will be available from your supplier. Briefly, the mould will be in three pieces, hull, deck, and cockpit-seat unit. Once these are clean and polished a layer of gel coat is applied and allowed to set touch dry. While the gel coat is curing the mat is cut into appropriately shaped pieces to fit into the mould. Lay-up resin is painted into the mould and the first layer of mat wetted into it with extra resin stippled into dry patches if necessary. This is repeated with the second layer of mat, taking care to cover the joints in the first layer by staggering the second.

Hull and deck are joined together with strips of mat applied through the cockpit hole with the mould held on each side in turn. The seat-cockpit unit is fitted into place with the hull-deck held almost upside down. It is usual to add some chalk filler to the resin used to joint the cockpit rim and deck. A stronger mix is obtained using an epoxy resin.

Various forms of strengthening are currently in use by commercial manufacturers – some have half round wooden moulding glassed in along the interior of the keel line, others use a hollow half round paper former for this and may use the same former for local strengthening of the deck. Many slalom craft are now strengthened with carbon fibres or a terylene-based cloth instead of glass mat. *Kevlar*, an aramid, gives an impact, tear and penetration resistance better than a similar glass mat lay-up but is currently approximately three times the cost of the equivalent glass.

Care must be taken to avoid the over-use of resin since, quite apart from its cost, this produces a heavy but not necessarily stronger craft.

In such a brief description of GRP canoe construction many details have been omitted and the prospective builder should read the literature available from suppliers, giving especial attention to safety in the use of glass fibre and the associated materials.

Building a plywood canoe

Building a plywood canoe on a mould was discussed on pp. 112–113. The traditional method when using plywood for boat construction was that of using it to cover a hard chine framework of frames and thin stringers. This is little used now that the 'stitch and glue' method has been introduced. Pre-cut panels of 3 mm or 4 mm plywood are 'sewn' together using short lengths of copper wire or nylon monofilament fishing line to form the stitches, the resulting joint being sealed with a laminate of glass tape and resin. This produces a hard or multi-chine hull, depending upon the number of panels. Kits or designs are currently available for building both kayaks and canoes.

In the early 1960s I used a development of this method to produce a round bilge hull shape without the need for moulds, building boards or jigs. The method involves cutting two plywood panels, one for each side of the hull, with a curved keel line. These two panels are then glued and nailed – using *Gripfast* boat nails – to a keelson so the curved keel lines come together along the centre line of the keelson. The result at this stage is a shallow saucer shape, curved both along the length of the hull and across the beam. Full length gunwale strips are glued and pinned along the gunwale line of each panel and the gunwales are drawn together to fit a pair of deck beams – the only other internal framing. The hull now resembles a canoe with the ends open beyond where the panels are fastened to the keelson. The ends are then 'stitched' together with copper wire or nylon monofilament fishing line and the joint sealed and reinforced with glass tape and resin. The hull is now complete, ready for internal finishing.

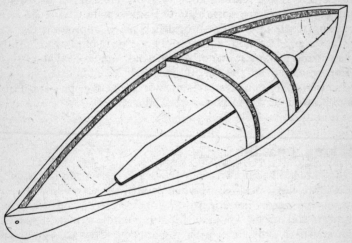

FIG. 13

A plywood hull of a DK design showing the keelson, two gunwale strips, and the two deck beams.

The deck is fitted in two parts by placing a second sheet of plywood over the front of the hull and marking around the edge, cutting out this fore deck and then repeating the process for the stern deck. The decks are glued and nailed to the gunwale strips and the deck beams. The gunwales are finished by rounding with a rasp or plane and covering with glass tape and resin. This effectively seals the edges of the hull and deck plywood. All that remains to be done is to build up the laminated cockpit coaming with off-cuts of plywood. A plywood seat can be fitted to the keelson or hung from the cockpit coaming. It is also possible to fit a GRP seat in this way.

If rough use is anticipated, the bottom of the hull can be clad with a layer of thin glass cloth and resin in the same way as the gunwales are protected with glass tape. The resulting craft has a strong, resilient monocoque hull which may be strengthened by adding GRP where necessary. The decks may be similarly strengthened or a thicker plywood can be used – 4 mm instead of 3 mm – where sea use is anticipated.

At present five adult DK designs are available, four single seat, and one two seat, each of which requires two 2.4 metres × 1.2 metres (8 feet × 4 feet) sheets of 3 mm thick exterior or marine grade plywood. There is also a junior single seat design for children weighing to about 40 kilos (100 lb). This is approximately 2.4 metres long (8 feet) and requires only one sheet of plywood for its construction making it one of the cheapest canoes available!

Further details of the DK designs may be obtained from the author on receipt of a stamped and addressed envelope – enquiries may be made via the publisher. See addresses p. 121

Making a paddle

If you have built your own canoe there is no reason why you should not make a single or double bladed paddle, too. Economically this may not be worthwhile for paddle kits represent good value, but with care and careful workmanship it is possible to make a wooden paddle which will show a saving in cost over its equivalent commercial product and gives the satisfaction of being self made.

A simple double bladed paddle is easily made by glueing and pinning a pair of plywood blades to a shaped length of light softwood.

Laminated paddles are rather more complicated to make and before attempting this I would suggest that you have a look at as many of this type of paddle as you can to see how the commercial manufacturer goes about it. This may well put you off the whole project for some of these paddles are beautiful examples of woodwork all too rarely seen in these days of plastics.

However, if you are still keen to have a go you will need a number of cramps for laminating the loom and possibly a mould for the

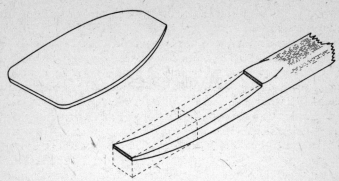

FIG. 14

How to shape the loom ends, and plywood blades for a simple double bladed paddle. Paddle blade 450 × 200 mm; loom 30 × 30 mm; length to suit.

blades if they are to be spooned. The scarf joint in the centre of the loom is to bring the laminations, which make up the loom, into the correct position to withstand the pressures applied by the paddler when using the paddle.

Paddle making sometimes becomes a hobby in itself and some amateurs are able to achieve the exact combination of strength and 'feel' in their paddles; at this point the sheer pleasure of making and using your own paddle overcomes any financial considerations.

Other equipment

Most of the other equipment you will require can be home-made.

Spray decks are an obvious example if a sewing machine is available.

A *folding trolley* for portageing is not difficult to construct (or a non-folding version might be designed to fit on the rear deck of a touring kayak).

Other possibilities will occur to you or be seen during your canoe travels.

Addresses

This is obviously not an exhaustive list but is intended to give you, the reader, some insight into the canoeing world and the opportunity to enquire further if you wish. Do remember to enclose a self addressed and stamped envelope with all enquiries.

British Canoe Union
Flexel House, 45–47 High Street, Addlestone, Weybridge, Surrey, KT15 1JV

The Canadian Canoe Association of Great Britain
Hon. Sec., Gable Cottage, Downs End, Leatherhead, Surrey, KT22 8JJ

Canoe Camping Club
11 Lower Grosvenor Place, London, SW1W 0EY

The Boys' Brigade
Brigade House, Parsons Green, London, SW6 4TH

The Girl Guides Association
17–19 Buckingham Palace Road, London, SW1W 0PT

The Scout Association
Baden-Powell House, Queensgate, London, SW7 5JS

British Waterways Board
Melbury House, Melbury Terrace, London, NW1 6JX

The following can supply details of courses in canoeing:

The Sports Council
70 Brompton Road, London, SW3 1EX

The Sports Council for Wales
Sophia Gardens, Cardiff

The Scottish Sports Council
1 St Colme Street, Edinburgh, EH3 6AA

The Sports Council for Northern Ireland
49 Malone Road, Belfast

DK plywood kayak plans:

Dennis Davis,
c/o Teach Yourself Books,
Hodder & Stoughton Paperbacks, 47 Bedford Square,
London, WC1B 3DP

Sticky repair tape, kayaks, canoes
McNulty Seaglass Ltd.,
Victoria Road, South Shields, Tyne & Wear

GRP materials and moulds

Prima Glassfibre Materials Ltd.,
Platts Eyot, Hampton, Middlesex, TW12 2HF

Strand Glassfibre
Brentway Trading Estate, Brentford, Middlesex

Trylon Ltd.,
Wollaston, Northants, NN9 7QJ

WEST System Epoxy,
York Street, Cowes, Isle of Wight, PO31 7BS

Addresses of other manufacturers will be found in current issues of canoeing magazines.

Canoeing journals

The Canoe-Camper – free to members of the Canoe Camping Club, also available on subscription.

Canoe Focus – free to members of the BCU.

Canoeing Magazine – monthly, available on subscription and some newsagents. Ocean Publications Ltd., 34 Buckingham Palace Road, London, SW1W 0RE

Bibliography

The books listed here are those I have personal knowledge of. Many are now out of print, some may be counted as 'collectors' items, while a few have been published in several editions; most will contain something of interest for the keen canoeist. Not all can be unreservedly recommended but those marked with an asterisk are of particular technical interest, and, being of recent publication, should be available from bookshops, or, if now out of print, from your public library. The BCU, in addition to publishing an excellent range of booklets on the various aspects of canoeing, also sell books and will supply a current list on request. Finally, as a collector, I am always delighted to be offered books on or about canoeing . . . !

*American Red Cross, *Canoeing*, Doubleday, N.Y., 1st ed. 1956
Anderson, R. C., *Canoeing & Camping Adventures*, C. Gilbert-Wood, 1910
Anon, *Kayak Canoeing*, 'Know the Game' Series, EP Publishing, 1st ed. 1973
*Barlow, F., *The Spur Book of Wild Water Canoeing*, Spurbooks, 1st ed. 1978
Barnes, E., *As the Water Flows*, Grant Richards, 1st ed. 1920
Blandford, P. W., *Canoeing*, Foyles Handbooks, 1st ed. 1957
Blandford, P. W., *Canoes & Canoeing*, Lutterworth Press, 1st ed. 1962

Blandford, P. W., *Canoeing Waters*, Lutterworth Press, 1st ed. 1966

Bliss, W., *Canoeing*, Methuen, 1st ed. 1934

Bliss, W., *Rapid Rivers*, Witherby, 1st ed. 1935

Boumphrey, G., *Down River*, Allen & Unwin, 1st ed. 1936

BCU, *Guide to the Waterways of the British Isles*, BCU, 3rd ed. 1960

BCU, Booklets on various aspects of canoeing

*Byde, A., *Living Canoeing*, A. & C. Black, 1st ed. 1969

Cattell, R. B., *Under Sail through Red Devon*, Maclehose, 1st ed. 1937

Chenu, C. M. *My Canoe*, Eric Partridge, 1st English ed. 1931

Cock, O. J., *You & Your Canoe*, Benn, 1st ed. 1956

* Davis, D. J., *The Book of Canoeing*, Arthur Baker, 1st ed. 1969

Davy, A., *4,000 Miles of Adventure*, Robert Hale, 1st ed. 1958

Downie, R. A., *The Heart of Scotland by Waterway*, Witherby, 1st ed. 1934

Dunnett, A. M., *Quest by Canoe: Glasgow to Skye*, Bell & Sons, 1st ed. 1950

*Duxbury, K., *Basic Coastal Navigation*, 'Know the Game' Series, EP Publishing, 1st ed. 1977

Ellis, A. R., *The Book of Canoeing*, Brown, Son & Ferguson, Glasgow, 1st ed. 1935

Ellis, A. R. & Beams, C. G., *How to Build & Manage a Canoe*, Brown, Son & Ferguson, 1st ed. 1949, vol. 1 text, vol. 2 plans

Fiennes Speed, H., *Cruises in Small Yachts and Big Canoes*, Norie & Wilson, 1883

Hayward, J. D., *Canoeing*, Bell & Sons, 1893

Helmericks, C., *We Live in Alaska*, Hodder & Stoughton, 1st ed. 1945

Henderson, J. L., *Kayak to Cape Wrath*, Maclellan, 1951

*Hutchinson, D., *Sea Canoeing*, A. & C. Black, 1st ed. 1975

Jagger, B., *Your Book of Canoeing*, Faber & Faber, 1st ed. 1963

Jessup, E., *The Boys' Book of Canoeing*, Dutton & Co. N.Y. 1st ed. 1926

Jones, M., *Canoeing Down Everest*, Hodder & Stoughton, 1st ed. 1979

Krustev, D., *River of the Sacred Monkey*, Wilderness Holidays, USA, 1st ed. 1970

Luscombe, W. G., *Canoeing*, Philip Allan, 1st ed. 1936

Luscombe, W. G., & Bird, L. J., *Canoeing*, A. & C. Black, 1st ed. 1936

McCarthy, R. H., *Canoeing*, Pitman's Games & Recreation Series, 1st ed. 1940

MacGregor, J., *A Thousand Miles in the Rob Roy Canoe*, Sampson Low, Marston, 1st ed. 1867

MacGregor, J., *The Rob Roy on the Jordan*, Murray, 1st ed. 1869

MacGregor, J., *The Rob Roy on the Baltic*, Sampson Low, Marston, 1st ed. 1872

McNaught, N., *The Canoeing Manual*, Nicholas Kaye, 1st ed. 1956

McNaught, N., *Canoe Cruising Manual*, Kaye & Ward, 1st ed. 1974

Mytton-Davies, P., *Canoeing for Beginners*, Elek Books, 1st ed. 1971

Paterson, R. M., *The Dangerous River*, Allen & Unwin, 1st ed. 1954

Pulling, A. V. S., *Elements of Canoeing*, Prakken Publishing Co. Michigan, 1st ed. 1933

Raven-Hart, Major R., *Canoe Errant*, John Murray, 1st ed. 1935

Raven-Hart, Major R., *Canoe Errant on the Nile*, John Murray 1st ed. 1936

Raven-Hart, Major R., *Canoe Errant on the Mississippi*, Methuen, 1st ed. 1938

Raven-Hart, Major R., *Canoe to Mandalay*, Frederick Muller, 1st ed. 1939

Raven-Hart, Major R., *Canoe in Australia*, Georgian House, Melbourne, 1st ed. 1948

Raven-Hart, Major R., *Canoeing in Ireland*, Canoe & Small Boat Ltd., n.d.

Rising, T. & T., *Kingfisher Abroad*, Cape, 1st ed. 1938

*Skilling, B., & Sutcliffe, D., (editors), *Canoeing Complete*, Nicholas Kaye, 1st ed. 1966

Squire, J. C., *Water-Music*, Heinemann, 1st ed. 1939

Steidle, R., *Wildwater Canoeing*, EP Publishing, 1st UK ed. 1977

Stevenson, R. L., *An Inland Voyage*, Chatto & Windus, 1st ed. 1890

Sutherland, C., *Modern Canoeing*, Faber & Faber, 1st ed. 1964

'Tiphys', *Practical Canoeing*, Norie & Wilson, 1883

Wilson, J., *Canoeing Down the Rhône*, Chapman & Hall, 1st ed. 1957

Index

MOUNTAINEERING

MIKE BANKS

Mountaineering is one of the most exciting and also one of the most exacting sports. Mike Banks here gives you all the background techniques which you need in order to climb safely and to become a competent all-round mountaineer.

As initial chapter on hill-walking is followed by advice on equipment and step-by-step instruction in rope-work and climbing technique, including snow and ice climbing, navigation, survival in bad conditions and rescue.

Mike Banks is an eminent and highly experienced mountaineer and polar explorer. In this book he not only communicates the skills he has learnt but puts across mountaineering as a deeply-rewarding and enjoyable sport.

TEACH YOURSELF BOOKS

FLY FISHING

MAURICE WIGGIN

This book provides simple guidelines for beginners and all fly fishermen newly addicted.

The object of this book is to encourage novices to take up their fishing rods with confidence and boldness. It covers every stage and technique of fly fishing, from building a rod through casting the fly to the grassing of the fish. The enthusiasm of the author, a well-known columnist on a national newspaper, is as delightful and instructive as is his encyclopaedic knowledge.

TEACH YOURSELF BOOKS

DINGHY RACING

BOB BOND

Dinghy sailing, whether at sea or on a reservoir, has become an increasingly popular sport, for weekends and summer evenings.

This book is for all those who have just acquired a boat or are thinking of going sailing. It gives the basics of the sport clearly and fully and will enable you to really teach yourself to sail. A particularly useful section is devoted to shore exercises which are designed to give a basic grounding in how a sailing boat works before you even go afloat.

Bob Bond is Training Manager to the Royal Yachting Association.

TEACH YOURSELF BOOKS